Patricia Wilson-Kastner

Inclusive-Language
Psalms

Inclusive-Language Psalms

from
An Inclusive-Language Lectionary

The Pilgrim Press
New York

Copyright © 1987 The Pilgrim Press
Copyright © 1983, 1984, 1985 Division of Education and Ministry,
National Council of the Churches of Christ in the U.S.A.

The psalms are from *An Inclusive-Language Lectionary (Readings for
Year A, B, and C),* copyright 1983, 1984, 1985 Division of Education
and Ministry, National Council of the Churches of Christ in the U.S.A.
and are used by permission.

PRINTED IN THE UNITED STATES OF AMERICA
9 8 7 6 5 4 3 2 1

Library of Congress Cataloging-in-Publication Data

Bible. O.T. Psalms. English. Revised Standard.
    Selections. 1987.
    Inclusive-language Psalms from Inclusive-language
lectionaries for years A, B, and C.

    "Lectionary texts are based on the Revised Standard
version of the Bible"—T.p. verso.
    Includes index.
    I. National Council of the Churches of Christ in
the United States of America. Inclusive Language
Lectionary Committee. II. Inclusive-language
lectionary. Readings for year A. III. Inclusive-
language lectionary. Readings for year B. IV. Inclusive-
language lectionary. Readings for year C. V. Title.
BS1436   1987   264'.34   87-2244
ISBN 0–8298–0747–0

The Pilgrim Press, 132 West 31 Street, New York, New York 10001

Contents

Introduction   vii

Psalms   1

Appendix   141

Index of Psalms by Sundays and Special Days   144

Index of Psalms for Church Years   147

Introduction

Praise GOD!
Praise God in the sanctuary;
Praise God in the mighty firmament! . . .
Let everything that breathes praise GOD!

The psalms have been used in Christian worship since New Testament times. They have served as scripture lessons and as hymns in corporate worship, including the graduals of the Roman Catholic Mass, and the metrical tunes of Protestant worship. The psalms also have had and continue to have an important place in private prayer and devotion.

This book contains all the psalms included in *An Inclusive-Language Lectionary* and is designed for both devotional and liturgical use. The psalms are taken from the Table of Readings and Psalms proposed by the North American Committee on Calendar and Lectionary, known as the *Common Lectionary. An Inclusive-Language Lectionary* was prepared by the Committee appointed by the Division of Education and Ministry of the National Council of the Churches of Christ in the U.S.A. Its task was to render the scripture readings from the *Common Lectionary* into gender-inclusive language and to reflect the inclusiveness of all persons. The Committee based its work on the Revised Standard Version of the Bible and the original Greek and Hebrew texts.

The psalms in this book are arranged in three basic formats:

- **Litanies.** Responsorial psalms arranged in litany form in which a leader reads the verses and the people answer with a response, printed in boldface type. All the psalms for basic Christian holy (feast) days, or festivals, are arranged in this way, as are some psalms for major penitential days in Lent and Holy Week.

- **Responsive readings.** All psalms except the responsorial psalms are arranged as responsive readings for corporate worship.

- **Unison readings.** A few of the psalms are printed for unison use in worship and appear on the same page as the psalm arranged for responsive reading. Worship leaders will determine which form is to be used.

Note to Worship Leaders

In this book "God [[*or* Lord]]" and "Sovereign [[*or* Lord]]" appear. Leaders need to direct worshipers as to which word is to be read. If "God" or "Sovereign" is used, "Lord" is *not* to be used.

The editorial committee for this book of psalms in inclusive language consists of Burton H. Throckmorton, Jr., Barbara A. Withers, and Jack H.

Haney, Editor. It is our hope that this book of psalms in inclusive language will lead persons and congregations to a deeper understanding of the God who is God of us all, in language that includes us all.

JACK H. HANEY
United Church Board for Homeland Ministries
Lent 1987

Psalm 1

¹ Blessed are those
who walk not in the counsel of the wicked,
nor stand in the way of sinners,
nor sit in the seat of scoffers,
² but whose delight is in the law of GOD [[or the LORD]],
and who meditate on that law day and night.

**Blessed are those whose delight
is in the law of God.**

³ They are like a tree
planted by streams of water,
that yields its fruit in its season,
and its leaf does not wither.
In all that they do, they prosper.

**Blessed are those whose delight
is in the law of God.**

⁴ The wicked are not so,
but are like chaff which the wind drives away.
⁵ Therefore the wicked will not stand in the judgment,
nor sinners in the congregation of the righteous;
⁶ for GOD [[or the LORD]] knows the way of the righteous,
but the way of the wicked will perish.

**Blessed are those whose delight
is in the law of God.**

EASTER 7
YEAR B
EPIPHANY 6
YEAR C

Psalm 2

1 Why do the nations conspire,
   and the peoples plot in vain?
2 The kings of the earth set themselves,
   and the rulers take counsel together,
   against GOD [[*or* the LORD]] and God's anointed, saying,
3 **"Let us burst their bonds asunder,**
   and cast their cords from us."
4 The One who sits in the heavens laughs,
   and has them in derision.
5 Then God will speak to them in anger,
   and terrify them in fury, saying,
6 "I have set my ruler□
   on Zion, my holy hill."
7 **I will tell of the decree of GOD [[*or* the LORD]]:**
   God said to me, "You are my child,
   today I have begotten you.
8 Ask of me, and I will make the nations your heritage,
   and the ends of the earth your possession.
9 You shall break them with a rod of iron,
   and dash them in pieces like a potter's vessel."
10 Now therefore, O kings, be wise;
   be warned, O rulers of the earth.
11 Serve GOD [[*or* the LORD]] with fear,
   with trembling 12 **kiss God's feet,**
   lest God be angry, and you perish in the way;
   for God's wrath is quickly kindled.

Unison:
   Blessed are all who take refuge in God.

□RSV *king.* See Appendix.

LAST SUNDAY AFTER EPIPHANY
YEAR A (Verses 6-11a)
EASTER 2
YEAR C

2

Psalm 3

1 O GOD [[or LORD]], how many are my foes!
Many are rising against me;
2 many are saying of me,
there is no help for that one in God.
3 But you, O GOD [[or LORD]], are a shield about me,
my glory, and the lifter of my head.
4 I cry aloud to GOD [[or the LORD]],
who answers me from God's holy hill.
5 I lie down and sleep;
I wake again, for GOD [[or the LORD]] sustains me.
6 I am not afraid of ten thousands of people
who have set themselves against me round about.
7 Arise, O GOD [[or LORD]]!
Deliver me, O my God!
For you smite all my enemies on the cheek,
you break the teeth of the wicked.
8 Deliverance belongs to GOD [[or the LORD]];
your blessing be upon your people!

PENTECOST 23
YEAR C

3

Psalm 4

1 Answer me when I call, O God of my right!
You gave me room when I was in distress.

Be gracious to me, and hear my prayer.

2 O people, how long shall my honor suffer shame?

How long will you love vain words, and seek after lies?

3 But know that GOD [*or* the LORD] has set apart the godly;

GOD [*or* the LORD] hears when I call.

4 Be angry, but sin not;

commune with your own hearts on your beds, and be silent.

5 Offer right sacrifices,

and put your trust in GOD [*or* the LORD].

6 There are many who say, "O that we might see some good!

Lift up the light of your countenance upon us, O GOD [*or* LORD]!"

7 You have put more joy in my heart

than they have when their grain and wine abound.

8 In peace I will both lie down and sleep;

for you alone, O GOD [*or* LORD], make me dwell in safety.

Psalm 5:1-8

1 Give ear to my words, O GOD [[*or* LORD]];
   give heed to my groaning.
2 Hearken to the sound of my cry,
   my Ruler[ ] and my God,
   for to you do I pray.
3 O GOD [[*or* LORD]], in the morning you hear my voice;
   in the morning I prepare a sacrifice for you, and watch.
4 For you are not a God who delights in wickedness;
   evil may not sojourn with you.
5 The boastful may not stand before your eyes;
   you hate all evildoers.
6 You destroy those who speak lies;
   GOD [[*or* the LORD]] abhors those who are bloodthirsty and deceitful.
7 But as for me, through the abundance of your steadfast love,
   I will enter your house;
   I will worship toward your holy temple
   in the fear of you.
8 Lead me, O GOD [[*or* LORD]], in your righteousness
   because of my enemies;
   make your way straight before me.

[ ]RSV *King.* See Appendix.

PENTECOST 7
YEAR C

5

Psalm 8

1 O SOVEREIGN, [[or LORD]], our God,
how majestic is your name in all the earth!
You whose glory above the heavens is chanted
2 by the mouth of babies and infants,
you have founded a bulwark because of your foes,
to still the enemy and the avenger.

**O SOVEREIGN, our God,
how majestic is your name in all the earth!**

3 When I look at your heavens, the work of your fingers,
the moon and the stars which you have established;
4 what are human beings that you are mindful of them,
and mortals that you care for them?

**O SOVEREIGN, our God,
how majestic is your name in all the earth!**

5 Yet you have made them little less than God,
and crowned them with glory and honor.
6 You have given them dominion over the works of your hands;
you have put all things under their feet,

**O SOVEREIGN, our God,
how majestic is your name in all the earth!**

7 all sheep and oxen,
and also the beasts of the field,
8 the birds of the air, and the fish of the sea,
whatever passes along the paths of the sea.

**O SOVEREIGN, our God,
how majestic is your name in all the earth!**

JANUARY 1 (NEW YEAR)
YEAR B
TRINITY
YEAR C

Psalm 9:11-20

¹¹ Sing praises to GOD [*or* the LORD], who dwells in Zion!
Tell among the nations the deeds of God!

¹² For the one who avenges blood is mindful of them,
and does not forget the cry of those who are afflicted.

¹³ Be gracious to me, O GOD [*or* LORD]!
Behold what I suffer from those who hate me,
O you who lift me up from the gates of death,

¹⁴ that I may recount all your praises,
that in the gates of beloved Zion
I may rejoice in your deliverance.

¹⁵ The nations have sunk in the pit which they made;
in the net which they hid has their own foot been caught.

¹⁶ GOD [*or* The LORD] has made God's self known and has executed judgment;
the wicked are snared in the work of their own hands.

¹⁷ The wicked shall depart to Sheol,
all the nations that forget God.

¹⁸ For the needy shall not always be forgotten,
and the hope of the poor shall not perish forever.

¹⁹ Arise, O GOD [*or* LORD]! Let no one prevail;
let the nations be judged before you!

²⁰ Put them in fear, O GOD [*or* LORD]!
Let the nations know that they are only human!

Psalm 10:12-18

12 Arise, O SOVEREIGN [[or LORD]]; O God, lift up your hand;
   forget not those who are afflicted.
13 Why does the wicked renounce God,
   and think, "You will not call to account"?
14 You see; you take note of trouble and vexation,
   that you may take it into your hands;
   those who have misfortune commit themselves to you;
   you have been the helper of the orphan.
15 Break the arm of the wicked and evildoer;
   seek out their wickedness till you find none.
16 GOD [[or The LORD]] is ruler⬚ forever and ever;
   the nations shall perish from God's land.
17 O GOD [[or LORD]], you will hear the desire of the meek;
   you will strengthen their heart, you will incline your ear
18 to do justice to the orphan and the oppressed,
   so that people who are of the earth may strike terror no more.

⬚RSV *king*. See Appendix.

Psalm 13

¹ How long, O God [*or* Lord]? Will you forget me forever?
How long will you hide your face from me?

² How long must I bear pain in my soul,
and have sorrow in my heart all the day?
How long shall my enemy be exalted over me?

³ Consider and answer me, O Sovereign [*or* Lord] my God;
lighten my eyes, lest I sleep the sleep of death;

⁴ lest my enemy say, "I have prevailed over you";
lest my foes rejoice because I am shaken.

⁵ But I have trusted in your steadfast love;
my heart shall rejoice in your salvation.

⁶ I will sing to God [*or* the Lord],
because God has dealt bountifully with me.

Psalm 14

¹ The foolish say in their heart,
   "There is no God."
   They are corrupt, they do abominable deeds,
   there is none that does good.

² GOD [*or* The LORD] looks down from heaven upon humankind,
   to see if there are any that act wisely,
   that seek after God.

³ They have all gone astray, they are all alike corrupt;
   there is none that does good,
   no, not one.

⁴ Have they no knowledge, all the evildoers
   who eat up my people as they eat bread,
   and do not call upon GOD [*or* the LORD]?

⁵ There they shall be in great terror,
   for God is with the generation of the righteous.

⁶ You would confound the plans of the poor,
   but GOD [*or* the LORD] is their refuge.

⁷ O that deliverance for Israel would come out of Zion!

Unison:

When GOD [*or* the LORD] restores the fortunes of God's people,
Jacob shall rejoice, Israel shall be glad.

Psalm 15

¹ O GOD [[*or* LORD]], who shall sojourn in your tent?
   Who shall dwell on your holy hill?
² The one who walks blamelessly, and does what is right,
   and speaks truth from the heart;
³ who does not slander with the tongue,
   and does no evil to a friend,
   nor takes up a reproach against a neighbor;
⁴ in whose eyes a reprobate is despised,
   but who honors those who fear GOD [[*or* the LORD]];
   who swears to one's own hurt and does not change;
⁵ who does not put out money at interest,
   and does not take a bribe against the innocent.

Unison:
   Whoever does these things shall never be moved.

PENTECOST 15
YEAR C

Psalm 16:5-11

5 GOD [[*or* The LORD]] is my chosen portion and my cup;
   you hold my lot.

6 The lines have fallen for me in pleasant places;
   I have a goodly heritage.

7 I bless GOD [[*or* the LORD]] who gives me counsel;
   in the night also my heart instructs me.

8 I keep GOD [[*or* the LORD]] always before me;
   because God is beside me, I shall not be moved.

9 Therefore my heart is glad, and my soul rejoices;
   my body also dwells secure.

10 For you do not give me up to Sheol,
   or let your godly one see the Pit.

11 You show me the path of life;
   in your presence there is fullness of joy,
   in your right hand are pleasures forevermore.

Psalm 17:1-7, 15

¹ Hear a just cause, O GOD [*or* LORD]; attend to my cry!
Give ear to my prayer from lips free of deceit!

² From you, let my vindication come!
Let your eyes see the right!

³ If you try my heart, if you visit me by night,
if you test me, you will find no wickedness in me;
my mouth does not transgress.

⁴ With regard to human works, by the word of your lips
I have avoided the ways of the violent.

⁵ My steps have held fast to your paths,
my feet have not slipped.

⁶ I call upon you, for you will answer me, O God;
incline your ear to me, hear my words.

⁷ Wondrously show your steadfast love,
**O savior of those who seek refuge
from their adversaries at your right hand.**

¹⁵ As for me, I shall behold your face in righteousness;
when I awake, I shall be satisfied with beholding your form.

Psalm 19:7-14

7 The law of GOD [[*or* the LORD]] is perfect,
   reviving the soul;
   the testimony of GOD [[*or* the LORD]] is sure,
   making wise the simple;
8 the precepts of GOD [[*or* the LORD]] are right,
   rejoicing the heart;
   the commandment of GOD [[*or* the LORD]] is pure,
   enlightening the eyes;
9 the fear of GOD [[*or* the LORD]] is clean,
   enduring forever;
   the ordinances of GOD [[*or* the LORD]] are true,
   and righteous altogether.
10 More to be desired are they than gold,
   even much fine gold;
   sweeter also than honey
   and drippings of the honeycomb.
11 Moreover by them is your servant warned;
   in keeping them there is great reward.
12 But who can discern one's errors?
   Clear me from hidden faults.
13 Keep back your servant also from presumptuous sins;
   let them not have dominion over me!
   Then I shall be blameless,
   and innocent of great transgression.

Unison:

14 **Let the words of my mouth and the meditation of my heart**
   be acceptable in your sight,
   O GOD [[*or* LORD]], my rock and my redeemer.

PENTECOST 17
YEAR A
LENT 3
YEAR B
EPIPHANY 3
YEAR C

14

Psalm 20

¹ May GOD [[*or* the LORD]] answer you in the day of trouble!
The name of the God of Jacob protect you!

² May God send you help from the sanctuary,
and give you support from Zion,

³ remembering all your offerings,
and regarding with favor your burnt sacrifices!

⁴ May God grant you your heart's desire,
and fulfill all your plans!

⁵ May we shout for joy over your victory,
and in the name of our God set up our banners!
May GOD [[*or* the LORD]] fulfill all your petitions!

⁶ Now I know that GOD [[*or* the LORD]] will help God's anointed,
and will answer the anointed one from God's holy heaven
with mighty victories by God's right hand.

⁷ Some boast of chariots, and some of horses;
but we boast of the name of the SOVEREIGN [[*or* LORD]] our God.

⁸ They will collapse and fall;
but we shall rise and stand upright.

⁹ Give victory to the ruler,□ O GOD [[*or* LORD]];
answer us when we call.

□RSV *king*. See Appendix.

Psalm 21:1-7

1 In your strength the monarch□ rejoices, O GOD [[*or* LORD]];
  and in your help how greatly the ruler exults!
2 You have satisfied the desire of the ruler's heart,
  and have not withheld the request of the ruler's lips.
3 For with goodly blessings you meet the monarch,
  upon whose head you set a crown of fine gold.
4 The ruler asked life of you; you gave it,
  length of days forever and ever.
5 Through your help, great is the glory of the monarch,
  upon whom you bestow splendor and majesty.
6 You make the ruler most blessed forever,
  glad with the joy of your presence.
7 For the monarch□ trusts in GOD [[*or* the LORD]],
  and through the steadfast love of the Most High shall not be moved.

□RSV *king*. See Appendix.

Psalm 22:1-18

¹ My God, my God, why have you forsaken me?
  Why are you so far from helping me, from the words of my groaning?
² O my God, I cry by day, but you do not answer;
  and by night, but find no rest.

My God, my God, why have you forsaken me?

³ Yet you are holy,
  enthroned on the praises of Israel.
⁴ In you our ancestors trusted;
  they trusted, and you delivered them.

My God, my God, why have you forsaken me?

⁵ To you they cried, and were saved;
  in you they trusted, and were not disappointed.
⁶ But I am a worm, not human at all;
  scorned by everyone, and despised by the people.

My God, my God, why have you forsaken me?

⁷ All who see me mock at me,
  they make mouths at me, they wag their heads and say,
⁸ "You trusted in GOD [[or the LORD]]; let God deliver you,
  let God rescue you, for God delights in you!"

My God, my God, why have you forsaken me?

⁹ Yet you, O God, are the one who took me from the womb;
  you kept me safe upon my mother's breasts.
¹⁰ Upon you I was cast from my birth,
  and since my mother bore me you have been my God.

My God, my God, why have you forsaken me?

¹¹ Be not far from me,
  for trouble is near
  and there is none to help.
¹² Many bulls encompass me,
  strong bulls of Bashan surround me;
¹³ they open wide their mouths at me,
  like a ravening and roaring lion.

My God, my God, why have you forsaken me?

(Continued on page 18)

¹⁴ I am poured out like water,
   and all my bones are out of joint;
   my heart is like wax,
   it is melted within my breast;
¹⁵ my strength is dried up like a potsherd,
   and my tongue cleaves to my jaws;
   you lay me in the dust of death.

My God, my God, why have you forsaken me?

¹⁶ Even dogs are round about me;
   a company of evildoers encircle me;
   they have pierced my hands and feet—
¹⁷ I can count all my bones—
   they stare and gloat over me;
¹⁸ they divide my garments among them,
   and for my raiment they cast lots.

My God, my God, why have you forsaken me?

GOOD FRIDAY
YEARS A, B, C

18

Psalm 22:25-31

25 From you comes my praise in the great congregation;
my vows I shall pay before those who fear God.
26 The afflicted shall eat and be satisfied;
those who seek God shall praise GOD [or the LORD]!
May your hearts live forever!

Those who seek God shall praise God!

27 All the ends of the earth shall remember
and turn to GOD [or the LORD];
and all the families of the nations
shall worship before God.
28 For dominion belongs to GOD [or the LORD],
who rules over the nations.

Those who seek God shall praise God!

29 Indeed, to God shall all the proud of the earth bow down;
before God shall bow all who go down to the dust,
and those who cannot keep themselves alive.

Those who seek God shall praise God!

30 Posterity shall serve God;
people shall tell of God [or the Lord] to the coming generation,
31 and proclaim God's deliverance to a people yet unborn,
that God has wrought it.

Those who seek God shall praise God!

Psalm 23

¹ GOD [[*or* The LORD]] is my shepherd, I shall not want;
² God makes me lie down in green pastures,
   and leads me beside still waters;
³ God restores my soul.

God is my shepherd, I shall not want.

   God leads me in paths of righteousness
   for God's name's sake.
⁴ Even though I walk through the valley of the shadow of death,
   I fear no evil;
   for you are with me;
   your rod and your staff,
   they comfort me.

God is my shepherd, I shall not want.

⁵ You prepare a table before me
   in the presence of my enemies;
   you anoint my head with oil,
   my cup overflows.

God is my shepherd, I shall not want.

⁶ Surely goodness and mercy shall follow me
   all the days of my life;
   and I shall dwell in the house of GOD [[*or* the LORD]]
   forever.

God is my shepherd, I shall not want.

LENT 4
YEAR A
EASTER 4
YEARS A, B, C
PENTECOST 27
YEAR A

Psalm 23

1 GOD [*or* The LORD] is my shepherd, I shall not want;
2 God makes me lie down in green pastures,
   and leads me beside still waters;
3 God restores my soul.
   God leads me in paths of righteousness
   for God's name's sake.
4 Even though I walk through the valley of the shadow of death,
   I fear no evil;
   for you are with me;
   your rod and your staff,
   they comfort me.
5 You prepare a table before me
   in the presence of my enemies;
   you anoint my head with oil,
   my cup overflows.
6 Surely goodness and mercy shall follow me
   all the days of my life;
   and I shall dwell in the house of GOD [*or* the LORD]
   forever.

LENT 4
YEAR A
EASTER 4
YEARS A, B, C
PENTECOST 27
YEAR A

Psalm 24

1 The earth is GOD's [or the LORD's] and the fullness thereof,
the world and those who dwell therein;

2 for God has founded it upon the seas,
and established it upon the rivers.

3 Who shall ascend the hill of GOD [or the LORD]?
And who shall stand in God's holy place?

4 Those who have clean hands and a pure heart,
who do not lift up their soul to what is false,
and do not swear deceitfully.

5 They will receive blessing from GOD [or the LORD],
and vindication from the God of their salvation.

6 Such is the generation of those who seek God,
who seek the face of the God of Jacob.

7 Lift up your heads, O gates!
and be lifted up, O ancient doors!
that the Ruler[□] of glory may come in.

8 Who is the Ruler[□] of glory?

GOD [or The LORD], strong and mighty,
GOD [or the LORD], mighty in battle!

9 Lift up your heads, O gates!
and be lifted up, O ancient doors!
that the Ruler[□] of glory may come in.

10 Who is this Ruler[□] of glory?

The GOD [or LORD] of hosts,
that one is the Ruler[□] of glory!

[□]RSV *King*. See Appendix.

ADVENT 4
YEAR A
PENTECOST 6
YEAR B
ALL SAINTS—NOVEMBER 1
YEAR B (Verses 1-6)
PRESENTATION—FEBRUARY 2
YEARS A, B, C (Verses 7-10, alternate)

Psalm 25:1-10

¹ To you, O GOD [[*or* LORD]], I lift up my soul.
² O my God, in you I trust,

let me not be put to shame;
let not my enemies exult over me.

³ Let none that wait for you be put to shame;

let them be ashamed who are wantonly treacherous.

⁴ Make me to know your ways, O GOD [[*or* LORD]];

teach me your paths.

⁵ Lead me in your truth, and teach me,

for you are the God of my salvation;

for you I wait all the day long.

⁶ Be mindful of your mercy, O GOD [[*or* LORD]],
and of your steadfast love,

for they have been from of old.

⁷ Remember not the sins of my youth, or my transgressions;

according to your steadfast love remember me,
for your goodness' sake, O GOD [[*or* LORD]]!

⁸ Good and upright is GOD [[*or* the LORD]],

who therefore instructs sinners in the way.

⁹ God leads the humble in what is right,

and teaches the humble God's way.

¹⁰ All the paths of GOD [[*or* the LORD]] are steadfast love and faithfulness,

for those who keep God's covenant and testimonies.

LENT 1
YEAR B
ADVENT 1
YEAR C

Psalm 26

1 Vindicate me, O GOD [[*or* LORD]], for I have walked in my integrity,
   and I have trusted in GOD [[*or* the LORD]] without wavering.
2 Prove me, O GOD [[*or* LORD]], and try me;
   test my heart and my mind.
3 For your steadfast love is before my eyes,
   and I walk in faithfulness to you.
4 I do not sit with those who are false,
   nor do I consort with dissemblers;
5 I hate the company of evildoers,
   and I will not sit with the wicked.
6 I wash my hands in innocence,
   and go about your altar, O GOD [[*or* LORD]],
7 singing aloud a song of thanksgiving,
   and telling all your wondrous deeds.
8 O GOD [[*or* LORD]], I love the habitation of your house,
   and the place where your glory dwells.
9 Sweep me not away with sinners,
   nor my life with those who are bloodthirsty,
10 in whose hands are evil devices,
   and whose right hands are full of bribes.
11 But as for me, I walk in my integrity;
   redeem me, and be gracious to me.
12 My foot stands on level ground;
   in the great congregation I will bless GOD [[*or* the LORD]].

Psalm 27:1-6

1 GOD [[*or* The LORD]] is my light and my salvation;
whom shall I fear?
GOD [[*or* The LORD]] is the stronghold of my life;
of whom shall I be afraid?

2 When evildoers assail me,
uttering slanders against me,
my adversaries and foes,
they shall stumble and fall.

3 Though a host encamp against me,
my heart shall not fear;
though war arise against me,
yet I will be confident.

4 One thing have I asked of GOD [[*or* the LORD]],
that will I seek after;
that I may dwell in the house of GOD [[*or* the LORD]]
all the days of my life,
to behold the beauty of GOD [[*or* the LORD]],
and to inquire in God's temple.

5 For God will hide me in a shelter
in the day of trouble,
and will conceal me under the cover of God's tent.
God will set me high upon a rock.

6 And now my head shall be lifted up
above my enemies round about me;
and I will offer in God's tent
sacrifices with shouts of joy;

Unison:
I will sing and make melody to GOD [[*or* the LORD]].

EPIPHANY 3
YEAR A (Verses 1-6)
PENTECOST 18
YEAR B (Verses 1-6)

25

Psalm 27:7-14

7 Hear, O GOD [[*or* LORD]], when I cry aloud,
be gracious to me and answer me!

8 You have said, "Seek my face."
My heart says to you,
"Your face, GOD [[*or* LORD]], do I seek."

9 Hide not your face from me.
Turn not your servant away in anger,
you who have been my help.
Cast me not off, forsake me not,
O God of my salvation!

10 For my father and my mother have forsaken me,
but GOD [[*or* the LORD]] will take me up.

11 Teach me your way, O GOD [[*or* LORD]];
and lead me on a level path
because of my enemies.

12 Give me not up to the will of my adversaries;
for false witnesses have risen against me,
and they breathe out violence.

13 I believe that I shall see the goodness of GOD [[*or* the LORD]]
in the land of the living!

14 Wait for GOD [[*or* the LORD]];
be strong, and let your heart take courage;
yes, wait for GOD [[*or* the LORD]]!

Psalm 28

1 To you, O GOD [[or LORD]], I call;
my rock, be not deaf to me,
lest, if you be silent to me,
I become like those who go down to the Pit.

2 Hear the voice of my supplication,
as I cry to you for help,
as I lift up my hands
toward your most holy sanctuary.

3 Take me not off with the wicked,
with those who are workers of evil,
who speak peace with their neighbors,
while mischief is in their hearts.

4 Requite them according to their work,
and according to the evil of their deeds;
requite them according to the work of their hands;
render them their due reward.

5 Because they do not regard the works of GOD [[or the LORD]],
or the work of God's hands,
God will break them down and build them up no more.

6 Blessed be GOD [[or the LORD]],
who has heard the voice of my supplications.

7 GOD [[or The LORD]] is my strength and my shield,
the one in whom my heart trusts;
so I am helped and my heart exults,
and with my song I give thanks to God.

8 GOD [[or The LORD]] is the strength of the people,
the saving refuge of God's anointed.

9 O save your people, and bless your heritage;
be their shepherd, and carry them forever.

PENTECOST 11
YEAR C

Psalm 29

1 Ascribe to God [[*or* the Lord]], O heavenly beings,
  ascribe to God [[*or* the Lord]] glory and strength.

2 Ascribe to God [[*or* the Lord]] the glory of God's name;
  worship God [[*or* the Lord]] in holy array.

3 The voice of God [[*or* the Lord]] is upon the waters;
  the God of glory thunders,
  God [[*or* the Lord]], upon many waters.

4 The voice of God [[*or* the Lord]] is powerful,
  the voice of God [[*or* the Lord]] is full of majesty.

5 The voice of God [[*or* the Lord]] breaks the cedars,
  God [[*or* the Lord]] breaks the cedars of Lebanon,

6 making Lebanon to skip like a calf,
  and Sirion like a young wild ox.

7 The voice of God [[*or* the Lord]] flashes forth flames of fire.

8 **The voice of God [[*or* the Lord]] shakes the wilderness,**
  God [[*or* the Lord]] shakes the wilderness of Kadesh.

9 The voice of God [[*or* the Lord]] makes the oaks to whirl,
  and strips the forests bare;
  and in God's temple all cry, "Glory!"

10 God [[*or* The Lord]] sits enthroned over the flood;
  God [[*or* the Lord]] sits enthroned as ruler□ forever.

11 May God [[*or* the Lord]] give strength to God's people!
  May God [[*or* the Lord]] bless the people with peace!

□RSV *king*. See Appendix.

Baptism of Jesus
Years A, B, C
Trinity
Year B

Psalm 30:4-12

⁴ Sing praises to GOD [[*or* the LORD]], O you saints of God,
  and give thanks to God's holy name.

⁵ For God's anger is but for a moment,
  and God's favor is for a lifetime.
  Weeping may tarry for the night,
  but joy comes with the morning.

⁶ As for me, I said in my prosperity,
  "I shall never be moved."

⁷ By your favor, O GOD [[*or* LORD]],
  you had established me as a strong mountain;
  you hid your face,
  I was dismayed.

⁸ To you, O GOD [[*or* LORD]], I cried;
  and to GOD [[*or* the LORD]] I made supplication:

⁹ "What profit is there in my death,
  if I go down to the Pit?
  Will the dust praise you?
  Will it tell of your faithfulness?

¹⁰ Hear, O GOD [[*or* LORD]], and be gracious to me!
  O GOD [[*or* LORD]], be my helper!"

¹¹ You have turned for me my mourning into dancing;
  you have loosed my sackcloth
  and girded me with gladness,

¹² that my soul may praise you and not be silent.
  O SOVEREIGN [[*or* LORD]] my God, I will give thanks to you forever.

Psalm 31:1-16

¹ In you, O GOD [*or* LORD], do I seek refuge;
let me never be put to shame;
in your righteousness deliver me!
² **Incline your ear to me,**
rescue me speedily!
Be a rock of refuge for me,
a strong fortress to save me!
³ You are my rock and my fortress;
for your name's sake lead me and guide me,
⁴ take me out of the net which is hidden for me,
for you are my refuge.
⁵ Into your hand I commit my spirit;
you have redeemed me, O SOVEREIGN [*or* LORD], faithful God.
⁶ You hate those who pay regard to vain idols;
but I trust in GOD [*or* the LORD].
⁷ I will rejoice and be glad for your steadfast love,
because you have seen my affliction,
you have taken heed of my adversities,
⁸ and have not delivered me into the hand of the enemy;
you have set my feet in a broad place.
⁹ Be gracious to me, O GOD [*or* LORD], for I am in distress;
my eye is wasted from grief,
my soul and my body also.
¹⁰ For my life is spent with sorrow,
and my years with sighing;
my strength fails because of my misery,
and my bones waste away.
¹¹ I am the scorn of all my adversaries,
a horror to my neighbors,
an object of dread to my acquaintances;
those who see me in the street flee from me.
¹² I have passed out of mind like one who is dead;
I have become like a broken vessel.

¹³ For I hear the whispering of many—
terror on every side!—

**as they scheme together against me,
as they plot to take my life.**

¹⁴ But I trust in you, O GOD [[*or* LORD]],

I say, "You are my God."

¹⁵ My times are in your hand;

deliver me from the hand of my enemies and persecutors!

¹⁶ Let your face shine on your servant;

save me in your steadfast love!

LENT 6, PASSION SUNDAY
YEARS A, B, C (VERSES 9-16)
EASTER 5
YEAR A (VERSES 1-8)

Psalm 32

¹ Blessed is the one whose transgression is forgiven,
whose sin is covered.

² Blessed is the person to whom GOD [[*or* the LORD]] imputes no iniquity,
and in whose spirit there is no deceit.

³ When I declared not my sin, my body wasted away
through my groaning all day long.

⁴ For day and night your hand was heavy upon me;
my strength was dried up as by the heat of summer.

⁵ I acknowledged my sin to you,
and I did not hide my iniquity;

**I said, "I will confess my transgressions to GOD [[*or* the LORD]]";
then you forgave the guilt of my sin.**

⁶ Therefore let all who are godly
offer prayer to you;

**at a time of distress, the rush of great waters
shall not reach them.**

⁷ You are a hiding place for me,
you preserve me from trouble;

you encompass me with deliverance.

⁸ I will instruct you and teach you
the way you should go;

I will counsel you with my eye upon you.

⁹ Be not like a horse or a mule, without understanding,
**which must be curbed with bit and bridle,
else it will not keep with you.**

¹⁰ Many are the pangs of the wicked;
but steadfast love surrounds the one who trusts in GOD [[*or* the LORD]].

¹¹ Be glad in GOD [[*or* the LORD]], and rejoice, O righteous,
and shout for joy, all you upright in heart!

EPIPHANY 6
YEAR B
PENTECOST 10
YEAR B

Psalm 33:1-22

1 Rejoice in GOD [[*or* the LORD]], O you righteous!
Praise befits the upright.

2 Praise GOD [[*or* the LORD]] with the lyre,
make melody on the harp of ten strings!

3 Sing to God a new song,
play skillfully on the strings, with loud shouts.

4 For the word of GOD [[*or* the LORD]] is upright;
and all God's work is done in faithfulness.

5 God loves righteousness and justice;
the earth is full of the steadfast love of GOD [[*or* the LORD]].

6 By the word of GOD [[*or* the LORD]] the heavens were made,
and all their host by the breath of God's mouth.

7 God gathered the waters of the sea as in a bottle,
and put the deeps in storehouses.

8 Let all the earth fear GOD [[*or* the LORD]],
let all the inhabitants of the world stand in awe!

9 For God spoke, and it came to be;
God commanded, and it stood forth.

10 GOD [[*or* The LORD]] brings the counsel of the nations to nought,
and frustrates the plans of the peoples.

11 The counsel of GOD [[*or* the LORD]] stands forever,
the thoughts of God's heart to all generations.

12 Blessed is the nation whose God is the SOVEREIGN [[*or* LORD]],
the people whom God has chosen as a heritage!

13 GOD [[*or* The LORD]] looks down from heaven,
and sees all humankind;

14 from where God sits enthroned God looks forth
on all the inhabitants of the earth,

15 God who fashions the hearts of them all,
and observes all their deeds.

(Continued on page 34)

¹⁶ A ruler⬚ is not saved by a great army;
   a warrior is not delivered by great strength.
¹⁷ The war horse is a vain hope for victory,
   and by its great might it cannot save.
¹⁸ The eye of the SOVEREIGN ⟦*or* LORD⟧ is on those who fear God,
   on those who hope in God's steadfast love,
¹⁹ that God may deliver their soul from death,
   and keep them alive in famine.
²⁰ Our soul waits for the SOVEREIGN ⟦*or* LORD⟧,
   who is our help and shield.
²¹ Indeed, our heart is glad in God,
   because we trust in God's holy name.
²² Let your steadfast love, O SOVEREIGN ⟦*or* LORD⟧, be upon us,
   even as we hope in you.

⬚RSV *king*. See Appendix.

TRINITY
YEAR A (Verses 1-12)
PENTECOST 2
YEAR A (Verses 12-22)
LENT 2
YEAR A (Verses 18-22)

Psalm 34

¹ I will bless GOD [[or the LORD]] at all times;
God's praise shall continually be in my mouth.

² My soul makes its boast in GOD [[or the LORD]];
let those who are afflicted hear and be glad.

³ O magnify GOD [[or the LORD]] with me
and let us exalt God's name together!

⁴ I sought GOD [[or the LORD]], who answered me,
and delivered me from all my fears.

⁵ Look to God, and be radiant;
so your faces shall never be ashamed.

⁶ This poor one cried, and GOD [[or the LORD]] heard me,
and saved me out of all my troubles.

⁷ The angel of GOD [[or the LORD]] encamps
around those who fear God,
and delivers them.

⁸ O taste and see that GOD [[or the LORD]] is good!
Happy is the one who takes refuge in God!

⁹ O fear GOD [[or the LORD]], you saints of God,
for those who fear God have no want!

¹⁰ The young lions suffer want and hunger;
but those who seek GOD [[or the LORD]] lack no good thing.

¹¹ Come, O children, listen to me,
I will teach you the fear of GOD [[or the LORD]].

¹² Which of you desires life,
and covets many days to enjoy good?

¹³ Keep your tongue from evil,
and your lips from speaking deceit.

¹⁴ Depart from evil, and do good;
seek peace, and pursue it.

¹⁵ The eyes of GOD [[or the LORD]] are toward the righteous,
and God's ears toward their cry.

(Continued on page 36)

¹⁶ The face of GOD [or the LORD] is against evildoers,
   to cut off the remembrance of them from the earth.
¹⁷ When the righteous cry for help, GOD [or the LORD] hears,
   and delivers them out of all their troubles.
¹⁸ GOD [or The LORD] is near to the brokenhearted,
   and saves the crushed in spirit.
¹⁹ Many are the afflictions of the righteous,
   but God [or the LORD] delivers them from their pain.
²⁰ God keeps all their bones;
   not one of them is broken.
²¹ Evil shall slay the wicked;
   and those who hate the righteous will be condemned.
²² GOD [or The LORD] redeems the life of God's servants;
   none of those who take refuge in God will be condemned.

ALL SAINTS—NOVEMBER 1
YEAR A (Verses 1-10)
PENTECOST 11
YEAR B (Verses 11-22)
LENT 4
YEAR C (Verses 1-8)

Psalm 35:17-28

17 How long, O God [[or Lord]], will you look on?

Rescue me from their ravages,
my life from the lions!

18 Then I will thank you in the great congregation;

in the mighty throng I will praise you.

19 Let not those rejoice over me
who are wrongfully my foes,

and let not those wink the eye
who hate me without cause.

20 For they do not speak peace,

but against those who are quiet in the land
they conceive words of deceit.

21 They open wide their mouths against me;

they say, "Aha, Aha!
our eyes have seen it!"

22 You have seen, O GOD [[or LORD]]; be not silent!

O God [[or Lord]], be not far from me!

23 Bestir yourself, and awake for my right,

for my cause, my God and my Sovereign [[or Lord]]!

24 Vindicate me, O SOVEREIGN [[or LORD]], my God,
according to your righteousness;

and let them not rejoice over me!

25 Let them not say to themselves,

"Aha, we have our heart's desire!"
Let them not say,

"We have swallowed that one up."

26 Let them be put to shame and confusion altogether
who rejoice at my calamity!

Let them be clothed with shame and dishonor
who magnify themselves against me!

(Continued on page 38)

²⁷ Let those who desire my vindication
  shout for joy and be glad,
  and say evermore,

  **"Great is GOD [[*or* the LORD]],
  who delights in the welfare of God's servant!"**

²⁸ Then my tongue shall tell of your righteousness
  and of your praise all the day long.

Psalm 36:5-10

⁵ Your steadfast love, O GOD [[*or* LORD]], extends to the heavens,
   your faithfulness to the clouds.
⁶ Your righteousness is like the mountains of God,
   your judgments are like the great deep;
   all living things you save, O GOD [[*or* LORD]].
⁷ How precious is your steadfast love, O God!
   All people may take refuge in the shadow of your wings.
⁸ They feast on the abundance of your house,
   and you give them drink from the river of your delights.
⁹ For with you is the fountain of life;
   in your light do we see light.
¹⁰ O continue your steadfast love to those who know you,
   and your salvation to the upright of heart!

EPIPHANY 2
YEAR C
MONDAY OF HOLY WEEK
YEARS A, B, C

Psalm 37:1-11

1 Fret not yourself because of the wicked,
   be not envious of wrongdoers!
2 For they will soon fade like the grass,
   and wither like the green herb.
3 Trust in GOD [[*or* the LORD]], and do good;
   so you will dwell in the land, and enjoy security.
4 Take delight in GOD [[*or* the LORD]],
   who will give you the desires of your heart.
5 Commit your way to GOD [[*or* the LORD]];
   trust in God, and God will act,
6 and will bring forth your vindication as the light,
   and your right as the noonday.
7 Be still before GOD [[*or* the LORD]], and wait patiently for God;
   fret not yourself over those who prosper in their way,
   over those who carry out evil devices!
8 Refrain from anger, and forsake wrath!
   Fret not yourself; it tends only to evil.
9 For the wicked shall be cut off;
   but those who wait for GOD [[*or* the LORD]] shall possess the land.
10 Yet a little while, and the wicked will be no more;
   though you look well at their place, they will not be there.
11 But the meek shall possess the land,
   and delight themselves in abundant prosperity.

EPIPHANY 4
YEAR A
EPIPHANY 7
YEAR C

40

Psalm 40:1-10

¹ I waited patiently for GOD [[*or* the LORD]],
who inclined to me and heard my cry.
² God drew me up from the desolate pit,
out of the miry bog,
and set my feet upon a rock,
making my steps secure.
³ God put a new song in my mouth,
a song of praise to our God.
Many will see and fear,
and put their trust in GOD [[*or* the LORD]].
⁴ Blessed is the one who
trusts in GOD [[*or* the LORD]],
who does not turn to the proud,
to those who go astray after false gods!
⁵ You have multiplied, O SOVEREIGN [[*or* LORD]] my God,
your wondrous deeds and your thoughts toward us;
none can compare with you!
Were I to proclaim and tell of them,
they would be more than can be numbered.
⁶ Sacrifice and offering you do not desire;
but you have given me an open ear.
Burnt offering and sin offering
you have not required.
⁷ Then I said, "I am coming;
in the scroll of the book it is written of me;
⁸ I delight to do your will, O my God;
your law is within my heart."
⁹ I have told the glad news of deliverance
in the great congregation;
I have not restrained my lips,
as you know, O GOD [[*or* LORD]].

(Continued on page 42)

¹⁰ I have not hid your saving help within my heart,
I have spoken of your faithfulness and your salvation;

**I have not concealed your steadfast love and your faithfulness
from the great congregation.**

Psalm 41

¹ Blessed are those who consider the poor!

GOD [[*or* The LORD]] delivers them in the day of trouble;

² GOD [[*or* the LORD]] protects them and keeps them alive;
they are called blessed in the land;

you do not give them up to the will of their enemies.

³ GOD [[*or* The LORD]] sustains them on their sickbed;

in their illness you heal all their infirmities.

⁴ As for me, I said, "O GOD [[*or* LORD]], be gracious to me;

heal me, for I have sinned against you!"

⁵ My enemies say of me in malice:

"When will that one die, and that name perish?"

⁶ And when people come to see me, uttering empty words,
their heart gathers mischief;

and when they go out, they tell it abroad.

⁷ All who hate me whisper together about me;

they imagine the worst for me.

⁸ They say, "A deadly thing has fastened upon that one,

who has lain down never to rise again."

⁹ Even my bosom friend in whom I trusted,

who ate of my bread, has betrayed me.

¹⁰ But you, O GOD [[*or* LORD]], be gracious to me,

and raise me up, that I may repay them!

¹¹ By this I know that you are pleased with me,

in that my enemy has not triumphed over me.

¹² But you have upheld me because of my integrity,

and set me in your presence forever.

¹³ Blessed be the SOVEREIGN [[*or* LORD]], the God of Israel,

from everlasting to everlasting!

Unison:

Amen and Amen.

EPIPHANY 7
YEAR B

Psalm 42

¹ As a hart longs
for flowing streams,
so longs my soul
for you, O God.
² My soul thirsts for God,
for the living God.
When shall I come and behold
the face of God?

**Hope in God; for I shall again praise God,
my help and my God.**

³ My tears have been my food
day and night,
while people say to me continually,
"Where is your God?"
⁴ These things I remember,
as I pour out my soul:
how I went with the throng,
and led them in procession to the house of God,
with glad shouts and songs of thanksgiving,
a multitude keeping festival.

**Hope in God; for I shall again praise God,
my help and my God.**

⁵ Why are you cast down, O my soul,
and why are you disquieted within me?
Hope in God; for I shall again praise God,
my help ⁶ and my God.
My soul is cast down within me,
therefore I remember you
from the land of Jordan and of Hermon,
from Mount Mizar.

**Hope in God; for I shall again praise God,
my help and my God.**

⁷ Deep calls to deep
   at the thunder of your cataracts;
   all your waves and your billows
   have gone over me.
⁸ By day GOD [[or the LORD]] commands God's steadfast love;
   and at night God's song is with me,
   a prayer to the God of my life.

**Hope in God; for I shall again praise God,
my help and my God.**

⁹ I say to God, my rock:
   "Why have you forgotten me?
   Why go I mourning
   because of the oppression of the enemy?"
¹⁰ As with a deadly wound in my body,
   my adversaries taunt me,
   while they say to me continually,
   "Where is your God?"
¹¹ Why are you cast down, O my soul,
   and why are you disquieted within me?

**Hope in God; for I shall again praise God,
my help and my God.**

Psalm 43

¹ Vindicate me, O God, and defend my cause
against an ungodly people;

**from deceitful and unjust people
deliver me!**

² For you are the God in whom I take refuge;
why have you cast me off?

**Why do I mourn
because of the oppression of the enemy?**

³ Oh send out your light and your truth;

let them lead me,

let them bring me to your holy hill

and to your dwelling!

⁴ Then I will go to the altar of God,

to God my exceeding joy;

and I will praise you with the lyre,

O God, my God.

⁵ Why are you cast down, O my soul,

and why are you disquieted within me?

Hope in God; for I shall again praise God,

my help and my God.

Psalm 44:1-8

1 We have heard with our ears, O God,
  our ancestors have told us,

  **what deeds you performed in their days,
  in the days of old:**

2 you with your own hand drove out the nations,

  but them you planted;

  you afflicted the peoples,

  but them you set free;

3 for not by their own sword did they win the land,

  nor did their own arm give them victory;

  but by your right hand, and your arm,
  and the light of your countenance;

  for you delighted in them.

4 You are my Ruler□ and my God,

  who ordains victories for Jacob.

5 Through you we push down our foes;

  through your name we tread down our assailants.

6 For not in my bow do I trust,

  nor can my sword save me.

7 But you have saved us from our foes,

  and have put to confusion those who hate us.

8 In God we have boasted continually,

  and we will give thanks to your name forever.

□RSV *King*. See Appendix.

Pentecost 6
Year C

Psalm 46

1 God is our refuge and strength,
  a very present help in trouble.
2 Therefore we will not fear though the earth should change,
  though the mountains shake in the heart of the sea;
3 though its waters roar and foam,
  though the mountains tremble with its tumult.

**God is our refuge and strength,
a very present help in trouble.**

4 There is a river whose streams make glad the city of God,
  the holy habitation of the Most High.
5 God is in the midst of it and it shall not be moved;
  God will help it right early.

**God is our refuge and strength,
a very present help in trouble.**

6 The nations rage, the kingdoms totter;
  God speaks, the earth melts.
7 The GOD [[or LORD]] of hosts is with us;
  the God of Jacob is our refuge.

**God is our refuge and strength,
a very present help in trouble.**

8 Come, behold the works of GOD [[or the LORD]],
  who has wrought desolations in the earth,
9 making wars cease to the end of the earth,
  breaking the bow, shattering the spear,
  and burning the chariots with fire!

**God is our refuge and strength,
a very present help in trouble.**

10 "Be still, and know that I am God.
  I am exalted among the nations,
  I am exalted in the earth!"
11 The GOD [[or LORD]] of hosts is with us;
  the God of Jacob is our refuge.

**God is our refuge and strength,
a very present help in trouble.**

PENTECOST 4
YEARS A, B

48

Psalm 47

¹ Clap your hands, all you people!
   Shout to God with loud songs of joy!
² For GOD [[or the LORD]], the Most High, is terrible,
   a great ruler⊡ over all the earth,

Alleluia! God has gone up with a shout.
Sing praises to God, sing praises!

³ subduing all people under us,
   and nations under our feet,
⁴ choosing our heritage for us,
   the pride of Jacob whom God loves.

Alleluia! God has gone up with a shout.
Sing praises to God, sing praises!

⁵ God has gone up with a shout,
   the SOVEREIGN [[or LORD]] with the sound of a trumpet.
⁶ Sing praises to God, sing praises!
   Sing praises to our Ruler,⊡ sing praises!

Alleluia! God has gone up with a shout.
Sing praises to God, sing praises!

⁷ For God is the ruler⊡ of all the earth;
   sing praises with a psalm!
⁸ God reigns over the nations,
   God sits on the holy throne.

Alleluia! God has gone up with a shout.
Sing praises to God, sing praises!

⁹ The nobles of the nations gather
   as the people of the God of Abraham.
   For the shields of the earth belong to God,
   who is highly exalted!

Alleluia! God has gone up with a shout.
Sing praises to God, sing praises!

⊡RSV vs. 2, 7 *king;* v. 6 *King.* See Appendix.

ASCENSION (or on EASTER 7)
YEARS A, B, C

Psalm 48

¹ Great is GOD [[or the LORD]] and greatly to be praised
in the city of our God!

God's holy mountain, ² beautiful in elevation,
is the joy of all the earth,

Mount Zion, in the far north,

the city of the great Ruler.⊡

³ Within its citadels God
has proven to be a sure defense.

⁴ **For lo, the rulers**⊡ **assembled,**
they came on together.

⁵ As soon as they saw it, they were astounded,

they were in panic, they took to flight;

⁶ trembling took hold of them there,

anguish as of a woman in travail.

⁷ By the east wind you shattered the ships of Tarshish.

⁸ **As we have heard, so have we seen**
in the city of the GOD [[or LORD]] of hosts,

in the city of our God,

which God establishes forever.

⁹ We have thought on your steadfast love, O God,

in the midst of your temple.

¹⁰ As your name, O God,

so your praise reaches to the ends of the earth.

Your right hand is filled with victory;

¹¹ **let Mount Zion be glad!**

Let the daughters of Judah rejoice

because of your judgments!

¹² Walk about Zion, go round about it,

number its towers,

¹³ consider well its ramparts,
go through its citadels;
that you may tell the next generation
¹⁴ **that this is God,**
our God forever and ever,
who will be our guide forever.

☐RSV v. 2 *King;* v. 4 *kings.* See Appendix.

Psalm 50:1-15

¹ The Mighty One, God the SOVEREIGN [[*or* LORD]],
speaks and summons the earth
from the rising of the sun to its setting.

² Out of Zion, the perfection of beauty,
God shines forth.

³ Our God comes and does not keep silence,
**before God is a devouring fire,
round about God a mighty tempest.**

⁴ God calls to the heavens above
and to the earth, in order to judge God's people:

⁵ "Gather to me my faithful ones,
who made a covenant with me by sacrifice!"

⁶ The heavens declare God's righteousness,
for it is God who judges!

⁷ "Hear, O my people, and I will speak,
O Israel, I will testify against you.
I am God, your God.

⁸ I do not reprove you for your sacrifices;
your burnt offerings are continually before me.

⁹ I will accept no bull from your house,
nor he-goat from your folds.

¹⁰ For every beast of the forest is mine,
the cattle on a thousand hills.

¹¹ I know all the birds of the air,
and all that moves in the field is mine.

¹² If I were hungry, I would not tell you;
for the world and all that is in it is mine.

¹³ Do I eat the flesh of bulls,
   or drink the blood of goats?
¹⁴ Offer to God a sacrifice of thanksgiving,
   and pay your vows to the Most High;
¹⁵ and call upon me in the day of trouble;
   "I will deliver you, and you shall glorify me."

LAST SUNDAY AFTER EPIPHANY
YEAR B (Verses 1-6)
PENTECOST 25
YEAR A (Verses 7-15)

Psalm 51:1-17

¹ Have mercy on me, O God, according to your steadfast love;
    according to your abundant mercy blot out my transgressions.
² Wash me thoroughly from my iniquity,
    and cleanse me from my sin!

Have mercy on me, O God.

³ For I know my transgressions,
    and my sin is ever before me.
⁴ Against you, you only, have I sinned,
    and done that which is evil in your sight,
    so that you are justified in your sentence
    and blameless in your judgment.

Have mercy on me, O God.

⁵ I was brought forth in iniquity,
    and in sin did my mother conceive me.
⁶ You desire truth in the inward being;
    therefore teach me wisdom in my secret heart.

Have mercy on me, O God.

⁷ Purge me with hyssop, and I shall be clean;
    wash me, and I shall be cleaner than snow.
⁸ Fill me with joy and gladness;
    let the bones which you have broken rejoice.
⁹ Hide your face from my sins,
    and blot out all my iniquities.

Have mercy on me, O God.

¹⁰ Create in me a clean heart, O God,
    and put a new and right spirit within me.
¹¹ Cast me not away from your presence,
    and take not your holy Spirit from me.
¹² Restore to me the joy of your salvation,
    and uphold me with a willing spirit.

Have mercy on me, O God.

13 Then I will teach transgressors your ways,
and sinners will return to you.
14 Deliver me from bloodguiltiness, O God,
the God of my salvation,
and my tongue will sing aloud of your deliverance.

Have mercy on me, O God.

15 O God [[or Lord]], open my lips,
and my mouth shall show forth your praise.
16 For you have no delight in sacrifice;
were I to give a burnt offering, you would not be pleased.
17 The sacrifice acceptable to God is a broken spirit;
a broken and contrite heart, O God, you will not despise.

Have mercy on me, O God.

ASH WEDNESDAY
YEARS A, B, C (Verses 1-12)
LENT 5
YEAR B (Verses 10-17)

55

Psalm 53

1 Fools say in their heart,
"There is no God."
They are corrupt, doing abominable iniquity;
there is none that does good.
2 God looks down from heaven
upon humankind
**to see if there are any that are wise,
that seek after God.**
3 They have all fallen away;
they are all alike depraved;
there is none that does good,
no, not one.
4 Have those who work evil no understanding,
**who eat up my people as they eat bread,
and do not call upon God?**
5 There they are, in great terror,
in terror such as has not been!
For God will scatter the bones of the ungodly;
they will be put to shame, for God has rejected them.
6 O that deliverance for Israel would come from Zion!
**When God restores the fortunes of God's people,
Jacob will rejoice and Israel be glad.**

Psalm 57

1 Be merciful to me, O God, be merciful to me,
for in you my soul takes refuge;

**in the shadow of your wings I will take refuge,
till the storms of destruction pass by.**

2 I cry to God Most High,

to God who fulfills God's purpose for me.

3 God will send from heaven and save me,
putting to shame those who trample upon me.

God will send forth God's steadfast love and faithfulness!

4 I lie in the midst of lions

that greedily devour their human prey;

their teeth are spears and arrows,

their tongues sharp swords.

5 Be exalted, O God, above the heavens!

Let your glory be over all the earth!

6 They set a net for my steps;

my soul was bowed down.

They dug a pit in my way,

but they have fallen into it themselves.

7 My heart is steadfast, O God,
my heart is steadfast!

I will sing and make melody!

8 Awake, my soul!
Awake, O harp and lyre!

I will awake the dawn!

9 I will give thanks to you, O God [[or Lord]], among the peoples;

I will sing praises to you among the nations.

10 For your steadfast love is great to the heavens,

your faithfulness to the clouds.

11 Be exalted, O God, above the heavens!

Let your glory be over all the earth!

Psalm 62:5-12

5 For God alone my soul waits in silence,
   for my hope is from God,
6 who alone is my rock and my salvation,
   my fortress;
   I shall not be shaken.
7 On God rests my deliverance and my honor;
   my mighty rock, my refuge is God.
8 Trust in God at all times, O people;
   pour out your heart before God,
   who is a refuge for us.
9 Those of low estate are but a breath,
   those of high estate are a delusion;
   in the balances they go up;
   they are together lighter than a breath.
10 Put no confidence in extortion,
   set no vain hopes on robbery;
   if riches increase, set not your heart on them.
11 Once God has spoken;
   twice have I heard this:
   that power belongs to God;
12 **and that to you, O God [[*or* Lord]], belongs steadfast love.**
   For you repay all people
   according to their work.

EPIPHANY 7
YEAR A
EPIPHANY 3
YEAR B

Psalm 63:1-8

¹ O God, you are my God, I seek you,
my soul thirsts for you;
my flesh faints for you,
as in a dry and weary land where no water is.
² So I have looked upon you in the sanctuary,
beholding your power and glory.
³ Because your steadfast love is better than life,
my lips will praise you.
⁴ So I will bless you as long as I live;
I will lift up my hands and call on your name.
⁵ My soul is feasted as with marrow and fat,
and my mouth praises you with joyful lips,
⁶ when I think of you upon my bed,
and meditate on you in the watches of the night;
⁷ for you have been my help,
and in the shadow of your wings I sing for joy.
⁸ My soul clings to you;
your right hand upholds me.

Psalm 65

1 Praise is due to you,
  O God, in Zion;
  and to you shall vows be performed,

2 **O you who hear prayer!**
  To you shall all flesh come

3 on account of sins.
  **When our transgressions prevail over us,
  you forgive them.**

4 Blessed is the one whom you choose and bring near,
  to dwell in your courts!
  We shall be satisfied with the goodness of your house,
  your holy temple!

5 By dread deeds you answer us with deliverance,
  O God of our salvation,
  who are the hope of all the ends of the earth,
  and of the farthest seas;

6 who by your strength have established the mountains,
  being girded with might;

7 who still the roaring of the seas,
  **the roaring of their waves,
  the tumult of the people;**

8 so that those who dwell at earth's farthest bounds
  are afraid at your signs;
  **you make the outgoings of the morning and the evening
  to shout for joy.**

9 You visit the earth and water it,
  you greatly enrich it;
  the river of God is full of water;
  **you provide their grain,
  for thus you have prepared the earth.**

10 You water its furrows abundantly,
  settling its ridges,
  softening it with showers,
  and blessing its growth.

¹¹ You crown the year with your bounty;
   the tracks of your chariot drip with fatness.
¹² The pastures of the wilderness drip,
   the hills gird themselves with joy,
¹³ the meadows clothe themselves with flocks,
   the valleys deck themselves with grain,
   they shout and sing together for joy.

THANKSGIVING DAY
YEAR A
PENTECOST 24
YEAR C (Verses 1-8)

61

Psalm 66:8-20

8 Bless our God, O nations,
   let the sound of God's praise be heard,
9 who has kept us among the living,
   and has not let our feet slip.
10 For you, O God, have tested us;
   you have tried us as silver is tried.
11 You brought us into the net;
   you laid affliction on our loins;
12 you let people ride over our heads;
   we went through fire and through water;
   yet you brought us forth to a spacious place.
13 I will come into your house with burnt offerings;
   I will pay you my vows,
14 that which my lips uttered
   and my mouth promised when I was in trouble.
15 I will offer to you burnt offerings of fatlings,
   with the smoke of the sacrifice of rams;
   I will make an offering of bulls and goats.
16 Come and hear, all you who fear God,
   and I will tell what God has done for me.
17 I cried aloud to God,
   and God was extolled with my tongue.
18 If I had cherished iniquity in my heart,
   God [[*or* the Lord]] would not have listened.
19 But truly God has listened
   and has given heed to the voice of my prayer.
20 Blessed be God!
   You have not rejected my prayer
   nor removed your steadfast love from me!

Psalm 67

¹ May God be gracious to us and bless us
   and make God's face to shine upon us,
² that your way may be known upon earth,
   your saving power among all nations.
³ Let the people praise you, O God;
   let all the people praise you!
⁴ Let the nations be glad and sing for joy,
   for you judge the people with equity
   and guide the nations upon earth.
⁵ Let the people praise you, O God;
   let all the people praise you!
⁶ The earth has yielded its increase;
   God, our God, has blessed us.
⁷ God has blessed us;
   let all the ends of the earth fear God!

JANUARY 1 HOLY NAME OF JESUS;
SOLEMNITY OF MARY, MOTHER OF GOD
YEARS A, B, C
PENTECOST 14
YEAR B

EASTER 6
YEAR C

Psalm 68:1-10

¹ Let God arise, let God's enemies be scattered;
let those who hate God flee before God!

² As smoke is driven away, so drive them away;
as wax melts before fire,
let the wicked perish before God!

³ But let the righteous be joyful;
let them exult before God;
let them be jubilant with joy!

⁴ Sing to God, sing praises to God's name;
lift up a song to the one who rides upon the clouds,
whose name is Sovereign [[or Lord]], exult before God!

⁵ Parent* of the orphan and protector of widows
is God in God's holy habitation.

⁶ God gives the desolate a home in which to dwell,
and leads out the prisoners to prosperity;
but the rebellious dwell in a parched land.

⁷ O God, when you went forth before your people,
when you marched through the wilderness,

⁸ the earth quaked, the heavens poured down rain,
at the presence of God;
Sinai quaked at the presence of God,
the God of Israel.

⁹ Rain in abundance, O God, you shed abroad;
you restored your heritage as it languished;

¹⁰ your flock found a dwelling in it;
in your goodness, O God, you provided for the needy.

---

*RSV **Father.** See Appendix, Metaphor.

Easter 7
Year A

Psalm 69:6-15

⁶ Let not those who hope in you be put to shame through me,
O Sovereign [[*or* Lord]] GOD of hosts;

**let not those who seek you be brought to dishonor through me,
O God of Israel.**

⁷ For it is for your sake that I have borne reproach,

that shame has covered my face.

⁸ I have become a stranger to my family,

an alien to my mother's children.

⁹ For zeal for your house has consumed me,

and the insults of those who insult you have fallen on me.

¹⁰ When I humbled my soul with fasting,

it became my reproach.

¹¹ When I made sackcloth my clothing,

I became a byword to them.

¹² I am the talk of those who sit in the gate,

and the drunkards make songs about me.

¹³ But as for me, my prayer is to you, O GOD [[*or* LORD]].

**At an acceptable time, O God,
in the abundance of your steadfast love answer me.**

With your faithful help ¹⁴ rescue me

from sinking in the mire;

let me be delivered from my enemies

and from the deep waters.

¹⁵ Let not the flood sweep over me,
or the deep swallow me up,

or the pit close its mouth over me.

PENTECOST 8
YEAR A

65

Psalm 70

¹ Be pleased, O God, to deliver me!

O GOD [[*or* LORD]], make haste to help me!

² Let them be put to shame and confusion
who seek my life!

**Let them be turned back and brought to dishonor
who desire my hurt!**

³ Let them be appalled because of their shame

who say, "Aha, Aha!"

⁴ May all who seek you
rejoice and be glad in you!

**May those who love your salvation
say evermore, "God is great!"**

⁵ But I am poor and needy;

hasten to me, O God!

You are my help and my deliverer;

O GOD [[*or* LORD]], do not tarry!

WEDNESDAY OF HOLY WEEK
YEARS A, B, C

Psalm 71:1-12

¹ In you, O GOD [or LORD], do I take refuge;
    let me never be put to shame!
² In your righteousness deliver me and rescue me;
    incline your ear to me, and save me!

For you are my rock and my fortress, O God.

³ Be to me a rock of refuge,
    a strong fortress, to save me,
    for you are my rock and my fortress.
⁴ Rescue me, O my God, from the hand of the wicked,
    from the grasp of the unjust and the cruel.

For you are my rock and my fortress, O God.

⁵ For you, O God [or Lord], are my hope,
    my trust, O GOD [or LORD], from my youth.
⁶ Upon you I have leaned from my birth;
    you are the one who took me from my mother's womb.
    My praise is continually of you.

For you are my rock and my fortress, O God.

⁷ I have been as a portent to many;
    but you are my strong refuge.
⁸ My mouth is filled with your praise,
    and with your glory all the day.

For you are my rock and my fortress, O God.

⁹ Do not cast me off in the time of old age;
    forsake me not when my strength is spent.
¹⁰ For my enemies speak concerning me,
    those who watch for my life consult together,
¹¹ and say, "God has forsaken the one who trusted;
    pursue and seize the forsaken one,
    for there is no one to give deliverance."
¹² O God, be not far from me;
    O my God, make haste to help me!

For you are my rock and my fortress, O God.

EPIPHANY 4
YEAR C (Verses 1-6)
TUESDAY OF HOLY WEEK
YEARS A, B, C (Verses 1-12)

Psalm 72:1-14

¹ Give the ruler⊡ your justice, O God,
  and your righteousness to the royal heir!
² May the ruler judge your people with righteousness,
  and your poor with justice!
³ Let the mountains bear prosperity for the people,
  and the hills, in righteousness!
⁴ May the ruler defend the cause of the poor of the people,
  give deliverance to the needy,
  and crush the oppressor!
⁵ May the ruler live while the sun endures,
  and as long as the moon, throughout all generations!
⁶ May the ruler be like rain that falls on the mown grass,
  like showers that water the earth!
⁷ In the ruler's days may righteousness flourish,
  and peace abound, till the moon be no more!
⁸ May the ruler have dominion from sea to sea,
  and from the River to the ends of the earth!
⁹ May the foes of the ruler bow down,
  and the enemies lick the dust!
¹⁰ May the kings of Tarshish and of the isles render tribute,
  may the kings of Sheba and Seba bring gifts!
¹¹ May all kings bow down
  and all nations serve the ruler!
¹² For the ruler delivers the needy when they call,
  the poor and those who have no helper,
¹³ and has pity on the weak and the needy,
  and saves the lives of the needy.
¹⁴ The ruler redeems their lives from oppression and violence,
  and their blood is precious in the ruler's sight.

⊡RSV *king.* See Appendix.

ADVENT 2
YEAR A (Verses 1-8)
EPIPHANY
YEARS A, B, C (Verses 1-14)

Psalm 76

¹ In Judah God is known,
  God's name is great in Israel.
² God's abode has been established in Salem,
  God's dwelling place in Zion.
³ There God broke the flashing arrows,
  the shield, the sword, and the weapons of war.
⁴ Glorious are you,
  more majestic than the everlasting mountains.
⁵ The stouthearted were stripped of their spoil;
  they sank into sleep;
  all the warriors
  were unable to use their hands.
⁶ At your rebuke, O God of Jacob,
  both rider and horse lay stunned.
⁷ But you, terrible are you!
  Who can stand before you
  when once your anger is roused?
⁸ From the heavens you did utter judgment;
  the earth feared and was still,
⁹ when God arose to establish judgment
  to save all the oppressed of the earth.
¹⁰ Surely the wrath of humans shall praise you;
  the residue of wrath you will gird upon you.
¹¹ Make your vows to the Sovereign [[*or* Lord]] your God,
  and perform them;
  let all around God bring gifts
  to God who is to be feared,
¹² who cuts off the spirit of princes,
  who is terrible to the kings of the earth.

Pentecost 26
Year A

Psalm 77:11-20

¹¹ I will call to mind the deeds of GOD [[*or* the LORD]];
I will remember your wonders of old.

¹² I will meditate on all your work,
and muse on your mighty deeds.

¹³ Your way, O God, is holy.
What god is great like our God?

¹⁴ You are the God who works wonders,
who has manifested your might among the nations.

¹⁵ With your arm you redeemed your people,
the offspring of Jacob and Joseph.

¹⁶ When the waters saw you, O God,
when the waters saw you, they were afraid;
the deep trembled.

¹⁷ The clouds poured out water;
the skies gave forth thunder;
your arrows flashed on every side.

¹⁸ The crash of your thunder was in the whirlwind;
you lightnings lighted up the world;
the earth trembled and shook.

¹⁹ Your way was through the sea,
your path through the great waters;
yet your footprints were unseen.

²⁰ You led your people like a flock
by the hand of Moses and Aaron.

Psalm 78:1-3, 10-20, 34-38

1 Give ear, O my people, to my teaching;
  incline your ears to the words of my mouth!
2 I will open my mouth in a parable;
  I will utter obscure sayings from of old,
3 things that we have heard and known,
  that our ancestors have told us.
10 They did not keep God's covenant,
  but refused to walk according to God's law.
11 They forgot what God had done,
  and the miracles that God had shown them.
12 In the sight of their ancestors God wrought marvels
  in the land of Egypt, in the fields of Zoan.
13 God divided the sea and let them pass through it,
  and made the waters stand like a heap.
14 In the daytime God led them with a cloud,
  and all the night with a fiery light.
15 God cleft rocks in the wilderness,
  and gave them drink abundantly as from the deep.
16 God made streams come out of the rock,
  and caused waters to flow down like rivers.
17 Yet they sinned still more against God,
  rebelling against the Most High in the desert.
18 They tested God in their heart
  by demanding the food they craved.
19 They spoke against God, saying,
  "Can God spread a table in the wilderness?
20 God smote the rock so that water gushed out
  and streams overflowed.
  Can God also give bread,
  or provide meat for God's people?"
34 When God slew them, they sought for God;
  they repented and sought God earnestly.

(Continued on page 72)

³⁵ They remembered that God was their rock,
the Most High God their redeemer.

³⁶ But they flattered God with their mouths;
they lied to God with their tongues.

³⁷ Their heart was not steadfast toward God;
they were not true to God's covenant.

³⁸ Yet God, being compassionate,
forgave their iniquity,
and did not destroy them,
restraining God's anger often,
and not arousing all God's wrath.

PENTECOST 13
YEAR A (Verses 1-3, 10-20)
HOLY CROSS—SEPTEMBER 14
YEARS A, B, C (Verses 1-2, 34-38—alternate)

Psalm 80:1-7

1 Give ear, O Shepherd of Israel,
  you who lead Joseph like a flock!

You who are enthroned upon the cherubim, shine forth
2 **before Ephraim and Benjamin and Manasseh!**

  Stir up your might,

  and come to save us!

3 Restore us, O God;

  let your face shine, that we may be saved!

4 O SOVEREIGN [[*or* LORD]] God of hosts,

  how long will you be angry with your people's prayers?

5 You have fed them with the bread of tears,

  and given them tears to drink in full measure.

6 You make us the scorn of our neighbors;

  and our enemies laugh among themselves.

7 Restore us, O God of hosts;

  let your face shine, that we may be saved!

ADVENT 1
YEAR B
ADVENT 4
YEAR C

Psalm 81:1-10

¹ Sing aloud to God our strength;
   shout for joy to the God of Jacob!
² Raise a song, sound the timbrel,
   the sweet lyre with the harp.
³ Blow the trumpet at the new moon,
   at the full moon, on our feast day.
⁴ For it is a statute for Israel,
   an ordinance of the God of Jacob.
⁵ God made it a decree in Joseph,
   when God when out over the land of Egypt.
   I hear a voice I had not known:
⁶ **"I relieved your shoulder of the burden;**
   your hands were freed from the basket.
⁷ In distress you called, and I delivered you;
   I answered you in the secret place of thunder;
   I tested you at the waters of Meribah.
⁸ Hear, O my people, while I admonish you!
   O Israel, if you would but listen to me!
⁹ There shall be no strange god among you;
   you shall not bow down to a foreign god.
¹⁰ I am the SOVEREIGN [[*or* LORD]] your God,
   who brought you up out of the land of Egypt.
   Open your mouth wide, and I will fill it."

Psalm 82

1 God stands up in the divine council;
 in the midst of the gods, God holds judgment:
2 "How long will you judge unjustly
 and show partiality to the wicked?
3 Give justice to the weak and the orphan;
 maintain the right of the afflicted and the destitute.
4 Rescue the weak and the needy;
 deliver them from the hand of the wicked."
5 They have neither knowledge nor understanding,
 they walk about in confusion;
 all the foundations of the earth are shaken.
6 I say, "You are gods,
 offspring of the Most High, all of you;
7 nevertheless, you shall die like human beings,
 and fall like any ruler."
8 Arise, O God, judge the earth;
 for to you belong all the nations!

PENTECOST 26
YEAR C

Psalm 84

¹ How lovely is your dwelling place,
  O GOD [[*or* LORD]] of hosts!
² My soul longs, even faints
  for the courts of GOD [[*or* the LORD]];
  my heart and flesh sing for joy
  to the living God.

How lovely is your dwelling place,
O God of hosts!

³ Even the sparrow finds a home,
  and the swallow a nest for herself,
  where she may lay her young,
  at your altars, O GOD [[*or* LORD]] of hosts,
  my Ruler⬚ and my God.

How lovely is your dwelling place,
O God of hosts!

⁴ Blessed are those who dwell in your house,
  ever singing your praise!
⁵ Blessed are those whose strength is in you,
  in whose heart are the highways to Zion.

How lovely is your dwelling place,
O God of hosts!

⁶ As they go through the valley of Baca
  they make it a place of springs;
  the early rain also covers it with pools.
⁷ They go from strength to strength;
  the God of gods will be seen in Zion.
⁸ O SOVEREIGN [[*or* LORD]] God of hosts, hear my prayer;
  give ear, O God of Jacob!

How lovely is your dwelling place,
O God of hosts!

⬚RSV *King.* See Appendix.

⁹ Behold our shield, O God;
  look upon the face of your anointed!
¹⁰ For a day in your courts is better
  than a thousand elsewhere.
  I would rather be a doorkeeper in the house of my God
  than dwell in the tents of wickedness.

**How lovely is your dwelling place,
O God of hosts!**

¹¹ For the SOVEREIGN [[*or* LORD]] God is a sun and shield,
  who bestows favor and honor.
  No good thing does GOD [[*or* the LORD]] withhold
  from those who walk uprightly.
¹² O GOD [[*or* LORD]] of hosts,
  blessed is the one who trusts in you!

**How lovely is your dwelling place,
O God of hosts!**

PRESENTATION—FEBRUARY 2
YEARS A, B, C
PENTECOST 14
YEAR C

Psalm 85:8-13

8 Let me hear what God the SOVEREIGN [[or LORD]] will speak,
   for God will speak peace to God's people,
   to God's saints, to those who turn to God in their hearts.
9 Surely salvation is at hand for those who fear God,
   that glory may dwell in our land.
10 Steadfast love and faithfulness will meet;
   righteousness and peace will kiss each other.
11 Faithfulness will spring up from the ground,
   and righteousness will look down from the sky.
12 The SOVEREIGN [[or LORD]] will give what is good,
   and our land will yield its increase.
13 Righteousness will go before God,
   and make God's footsteps a way.

Psalm 89:1-4, 19-37

¹ I will sing of your steadfast love, O GOD [[or LORD]], forever;
  with my mouth I will proclaim your faithfulness to all generations.

² For your steadfast love was established forever,
  your faithfulness is firm as the heavens.

³ You have said, "I have made a covenant with my chosen one,
  I have sworn to David my servant:

⁴ 'I will establish your descendants forever,
  and build your throne for all generations.'"

¹⁹ Of old you spoke in a vision
  to your faithful one, and said:

  "I have set the crown upon one who is mighty,
  I have exalted one chosen from the people.

²⁰ I have found David, my servant;
  with my holy oil I have anointed him;

²¹ so that my hand shall ever abide with David,
  my arm also shall strengthen him.

²² The enemy shall not outwit him,
  the wicked shall not humble him.

²³ I will crush David's foes before him
  and strike down those who hate him.

²⁴ My faithfulness and my steadfast love shall be with him,
  and in my name shall David's horn be exalted."

²⁵ I will set his hand on the sea
  and his right hand on the rivers.

²⁶ He shall cry to me, "You are my Parent,*
  my God, and the Rock of my salvation."

²⁷ And I will make him the firstborn,
  the highest of the kings of the earth.

²⁸ My steadfast love I will keep for David forever,
  and my covenant will stand firm for him.

(Continued on page 80)

---

*RSV *Father.* See Appendix, Metaphor.

²⁹ I will establish David's line forever
  and his throne as the days of the heavens.
³⁰ If David's children forsake my law
  and do not walk according to my ordinances,
³¹ if they violate my statutes
  and do not keep my commandments,
³² then I will punish their transgression with the rod
  and their iniquity with scourges;
³³ but I will not remove from David my steadfast love,
  or be false to my faithfulness.
³⁴ I will not violate my covenant,
  or alter the word that went forth from my lips.
³⁵ Once for all I have sworn by my holiness;
  I will not lie to David,
³⁶ whose line shall endure forever,
  whose throne as long as the sun before me.
³⁷ Like the moon it shall be established forever;
  it shall stand firm while the skies endure.

ADVENT 4
YEAR B (Verses 1-4, 19-24)
PENTECOST 7
YEAR B (Verses 20-37)

Psalm 89:20-21, 24, 26

(Psalm 89:20-21, 24, 26, is used at the Chrism service of Maundy [Holy] Thursday.)

20 I have found David, my servant;
  with my holy oil I have anointed him;
21 so that my hand shall ever abide with David,
  my arm also shall strengthen him.
24 My faithfulness and my steadfast love shall be with him,
  and in my name shall David's horn be exalted.
26 He shall cry to me, "You are my Parent,*
  my God, and the Rock of my salvation."

---

*RSV **Father.** See Appendix, Metaphor.

Psalm 90:1-12

1 God [[or Lord]], you have been our dwelling place
    in all generations.
2 **Before the mountains were brought forth,**
    or ever you had formed the earth and the world,
    from everlasting to everlasting you are God.
3 You turn people back to the dust,
    and say, "Turn back, O mortals!"
4 For a thousand years in your sight
    are but as yesterday when it is past,
    or as a watch in the night.
5 You sweep people away; they are like a dream,
    like grass which is renewed in the morning:
6 in the morning it flourishes and is renewed;
    in the evening it fades and withers.
7 For we are consumed by your anger;
    by your wrath we are overwhelmed.
8 You have set our iniquities before you,
    our secret sins in the light of your countenance.
9 For all our days pass away under your wrath,
    our years come to an end like a sigh.
10 The years of our life are threescore and ten,
    or even by reason of strength fourscore;
    yet their span is but toil and trouble;
    they are soon gone, and we fly away.
11 Who considers the power of your anger,
    and your wrath according to the fear of you?
12 So teach us to number our days
    that we may get a heart of wisdom.

PENTECOST 21
YEAR B
JANUARY 1 (NEW YEAR)
YEAR C

Psalm 91

1 Whoever dwells in the shelter of the Most High,
who abides in the shadow of the Almighty,
2 will say to GOD [[*or* the LORD]], "My refuge and my fortress;
my God, in whom I trust."
3 For God will deliver you from the snare of the fowler
and from the deadly pestilence;
4 God will cover you with God's pinions,
and under God's wings you will find refuge;
God's faithfulness is a shield and buckler.
5 You will not fear the terror of the night,
nor the arrow that flies by day,
6 nor the pestilence that stalks at midnight,
nor the destruction that wastes at noonday.
7 A thousand may fall at your side,
ten thousand at your right hand;
but it will not come near you.
8 You will only look with your eyes
and see the recompense of the wicked.
9 Because you have made GOD [[*or* the LORD]] your refuge,
the Most High your habitation,
10 no evil shall befall you,
no scourge come near your tent.
11 For God will give the angels charge of you
to guard you in all your ways.
12 On their hands they will bear you up,
lest you dash your foot against a stone.
13 You will tread on the lion and the adder,
the young lion and the serpent you will trample underfoot.
14 Whoever clings to me in love, I will deliver;
I will protect the one who knows my name.
15 When that one calls to me, I will answer;
I will be present in trouble,
I will rescue and honor whoever calls.
16 With long life I will satisfy them,
and show forth my salvation.

PENTECOST 5
YEAR A (Verses 1-10)
LENT 1
YEAR C (Verses 9-16)

Psalm 92:1-4, 12-15

1 It is good to give thanks to GOD [[*or* the LORD]],
   to sing praises to your name, O Most High;

2 to declare your steadfast love in the morning,
   and your faithfulness by night,

3 to the music of the lute and the harp,
   to the melody of the lyre.

4 For you, O GOD [[*or* LORD]], have made me glad by your work;
   at the works of your hands I sing for joy.

12 The righteous flourish like the palm tree,
   and grow like a cedar in Lebanon.

13 They are planted in the house of the SOVEREIGN [[*or* LORD]],
   they flourish in the courts of our God.

14 They still bring forth fruit in old age,
   they are ever full of sap and green,

15 to show that GOD [[*or* the LORD]] is upright,
   my rock, in whom there is no unrighteousness.

Psalm 93

1 GOD [[*or* The LORD]] reigns, robed in majesty;
GOD [[*or* the LORD]] is robed, and girded with strength.

The world is established; it shall never be moved;
2 your throne is established from of old;
you are from everlasting.

3 The floods have lifted up, O GOD [[*or* LORD]],
the floods have lifted up their voice,
the floods lift up their roaring.

4 Mightier than the thunders of many waters,
mightier than the waves of the sea,
GOD [[*or* the LORD]] on high is mighty!

5 Your decrees are very sure;
holiness befits your house,
O GOD [[*or* LORD]], forevermore.

PENTECOST 27
YEAR B

Psalm 94:12-22

12 Blessed are those whom you chasten, O GOD [[or LORD]],
  and whom you teach out of your law

13 to give them respite from days of trouble,
  until a pit is dug for the wicked.

14 For GOD [[or the LORD]] will not forsake God's people,
  and will not abandon God's heritage;

15 for justice will return to the righteous,
  and all the upright in heart will follow it.

16 Who rises up for me against the wicked?
  Who stands up for me against the evildoers?

17 If GOD [[or the LORD]] had not been my help,
  my soul would soon have dwelt in the land of silence.

18 When I thought, "My foot slips,"
  your steadfast love, O GOD [[or LORD]], held me up.

19 When the cares of my heart are many,
  your consolations cheer my soul.

20 Can wicked rulers be allied with you,
  who frame mischief by statute?

21 They band together against the life of the righteous,
  and condemn the innocent to death.

22 But the SOVEREIGN [[or LORD]] has become my stronghold,
  and my God the rock of my refuge.

PENTECOST 16
YEAR C

Psalm 95

1 O come, let us sing to GOD [[*or* the LORD]];
let us make a joyful noise to the rock of our salvation!

2 Let us come into God's presence with thanksgiving;
let us make a joyful noise to God with songs of praise!

3 For the SOVEREIGN [[*or* LORD]] is a great God,
and a great Ruler⬚ above all gods.

4 The depths of the earth are in the hand of God;
the heights of the mountains are God's also.

5 The sea belongs to God, for God made it;
for God's hands formed the dry land.

6 O come, let us worship and bow down,
let us kneel before GOD [[*or* the LORD]], our Maker!

7 For this is our God,
and we are the people of God's pasture,
and the sheep of God's hand.
O that today you would hearken to the voice of God!

8 **Harden not your hearts, as at Meribah,**
as on the day at Massah in the wilderness,

9 when your ancestors tested me,
and put me to the proof, though they had seen my work.

10 For forty years I loathed that generation
and said, "They are a people who err in heart,
and they do not regard my ways."

11 Therefore I swore in my anger
that they should not enter my rest.

⬚RSV *King.* See Appendix.

LENT 3
YEAR A
PENTECOST 14
YEAR A
PENTECOST 27
YEAR C

Psalm 96

1 O sing to God a new song;
   sing to GOD [[or the LORD]], all the earth!
2 Sing to GOD [[or the LORD]], bless God's name.
   Tell of God's salvation from day to day.

Hallelujah!
O sing to God a new song.

3 Declare God's glory among the nations,
   God's marvelous works among all people!
4 For great is GOD [[or the LORD]], and greatly to be praised,
   indeed, to be feared above all gods.

Hallelujah!
O sing to God a new song.

5 For all the gods of the nations are idols;
   but the SOVEREIGN [[or LORD]] made the heavens.
6 Honor and majesty are before God;
   strength and beauty are in God's sanctuary.

Hallelujah!
O sing to God a new song.

7 Ascribe to GOD [[or the LORD]], O families of nations,
   ascribe to GOD [[or the LORD]] glory and strength!
8 Ascribe to GOD [[or the LORD]] the glory due God's name;
   bring an offering, and come into God's courts!

Hallelujah!
O sing to God a new song.

9 Worship GOD [[or the LORD]] in holy array;
   tremble before God, all the earth!
10 Say among the nations, "GOD [[or The LORD]] reigns!
    The world is established; it shall never be moved;
    God will judge the nations with equity."

Hallelujah!
O sing to God a new song.

¹¹ Let the heavens be glad, and let the earth rejoice;
   let the sea roar, and all that fills it;
¹² let the field exult, and everything in it!
   Then shall all the trees of the wood sing for joy
¹³ before GOD [[*or* the LORD]], who comes,
   who comes to judge the earth,
   who will judge the world with righteousness,
   and the nations with truth.

Hallelujah!
O sing to God a new song.

Psalm 97

¹ GOD [[*or* The LORD]] reigns; let the earth rejoice;
   let the many coastlands be glad!
² Clouds and thick darkness are round about God;
   righteousness and justice are the foundation of God's throne.

Hallelujah!
God reigns; let the earth rejoice.

³ Fire goes before God,
   and burns up God's adversaries round about.
⁴ God's lightnings lighten the world;
   the earth sees and trembles.
⁵ The mountains melt like wax before the SOVEREIGN [[*or* LORD]],
   before the God [[*or* Lord]] of all the earth.

Hallelujah!
God reigns; let the earth rejoice.

⁶ The heavens proclaim God's righteousness;
   and all people behold God's glory.
⁷ All worshipers of images are put to shame,
   who make their boast in worthless idols;
   all gods bow down before God.

Hallelujah!
God reigns; let the earth rejoice.

⁸ Zion hears and is glad,
   and the daughters of Judah rejoice,
   because of your judgments, O GOD [[*or* LORD]].
⁹ For you, O GOD [[*or* LORD]], are most high over all the earth;
   you are exalted far above all gods.

Hallelujah!
God reigns; let the earth rejoice.

¹⁰ GOD [[*or* The LORD]] loves those who hate evil,
  preserves the lives of the saints,
  and delivers them from the hand of the wicked.
¹¹ Light dawns for the righteous,
  and joy for the upright in heart.
¹² Rejoice in GOD [[*or* the LORD]], O you righteous,
  and give thanks to God's holy name!

Hallelujah!
God reigns; let the earth rejoice.

CHRISTMAS DAY, ADDITIONAL, FIRST SET
YEARS A, B, C
EASTER 7
YEAR C

Psalm 98

¹ O sing a new song to GOD [[*or* the LORD]],
who has done marvelous things,
whose right hand and holy arm
have gained the victory!
² GOD [[*or* The LORD]] has made known the victory,
and has revealed God's vindication in the sight of the nations.

Hallelujah!
O sing a new song to God.

³ God has remembered God's steadfast love and faithfulness
to the house of Israel.
All the ends of the earth have seen
the victory of our God.
⁴ Make a joyful noise to GOD [[*or* the LORD]], all the earth;
break forth into joyous song and sing praises!

Hallelujah!
O sing a new song to God.

⁵ Sing praises to GOD [[*or* the LORD]] with the lyre,
with the lyre and the sound of melody!
⁶ With trumpets and the sound of the horn
make a joyful noise before the Ruler,□ the SOVEREIGN [[*or* LORD]]!

Hallelujah!
O sing a new song to God.

⁷ Let the sea roar, and all that fills it;
   the world and those who dwell in it!
⁸ Let the floods clap their hands;
   let the hills sing together for joy
⁹ before GOD [[*or* the LORD]], for God comes
   to judge the earth,
   to judge the world with righteousness,
   and the nations with equity.

Hallelujah!
O sing a new song to God.

☐RSV *King*. See Appendix.

CHRISTMAS DAY, ADDITIONAL, SECOND SET
YEARS A, B, C
EASTER 6
YEAR B
HOLY CROSS—SEPTEMBER 14
YEARS A, B, C (Verses 1-5)

Psalm 99

¹ GOD [[*or* The LORD]] reigns; let all people tremble!
God sits enthroned upon the cherubim; let the earth quake!

² GOD [[*or* The LORD]] is great in Zion,
and is exalted over all the nations.

³ Let them praise your great and terrible name!
Holy is God!

⁴ Mighty Ruler,□ lover of justice,
you have established equity;
**you have executed justice
and righteousness in Jacob.**

⁵ Extol the SOVEREIGN [[*or* LORD]] our God;
worship at God's footstool!
Holy is God!

⁶ Moses and Aaron were among the priests of God,
Samuel also was among those who called on God's name.
They cried to GOD [[*or* the LORD]] who answered them,
⁷ **and spoke to them in the pillar of cloud.**
They kept God's testimonies,
and the statutes that God gave them.

⁸ O SOVEREIGN [[*or* LORD]] our God, you answered them;
**you were a forgiving God to them,
but an avenger of their wrongdoings.**

⁹ Extol the SOVEREIGN [[*or* LORD]] our God,
and worship at God's holy mountain;
for the SOVEREIGN [[*or* LORD]] our God is holy!

□RSV *King*. See Appendix.

PENTECOST 19
YEAR A
LAST SUNDAY AFTER EPIPHANY
YEAR C

Psalm 100

¹ Make a joyful noise to GOD [*or* the LORD], all the lands!
² **Serve GOD [*or* the LORD] with gladness!**
Come into God's presence with singing!
³ Know that the SOVEREIGN [*or* LORD] is God!
It is God who made us, and to God we belong;
we are God's people, and the sheep of God's pasture.
⁴ Enter God's gates with thanksgiving,
and God's courts with praise!
Give thanks to God, bless God's name!
⁵ For GOD [*or* the LORD] is good;
God's steadfast love endures forever,
and God's faithfulness to all generations.

Unison:
¹ **Make a joyful noise to GOD [*or* the LORD], all the lands!**
² **Serve GOD [*or* the LORD] with gladness!**
Come into God's presence with singing!
³ **Know that the SOVEREIGN [*or* LORD] is God!**
It is God who made us, and to God we belong;
we are God's people, and the sheep of God's pasture.
⁴ **Enter God's gates with thanksgiving,**
and God's courts with praise!
Give thanks to God, bless God's name!
⁵ **For GOD [*or* the LORD] is good;**
God's steadfast love endures forever,
and God's faithfulness to all generations.

PENTECOST 2
YEAR C
THANKSGIVING DAY
YEAR C

Psalm 101

¹ I will sing of loyalty and of justice;
to you, O GOD [[*or* LORD]], I will sing.

² I will give heed to the way that is blameless.
Oh when will you come to me?
I will walk with integrity of heart
within my house;

³ I will not set before my eyes
anything that is base.
I hate the work of those who fall away;
it shall not cleave to me.

⁴ Perverseness of heart shall be far from me;
I will know nothing of evil.

⁵ The one who slanders a neighbor secretly
I will destroy.
The one of haughty looks and arrogant heart
I will not endure.

⁶ I will look with favor on the faithful in the land,
that they may dwell with me;
one who walks in the way that is blameless
shall minister to me.

⁷ No one who practices deceit
shall dwell in my house;
no one who utters lies
shall continue in my presence.

⁸ Morning by morning I will destroy
all the wicked in the land,
cutting off all the evildoers
from the city of GOD [[*or* the LORD]].

PENTECOST 20
YEAR C

Psalm 102:1-12

¹ Hear my prayer, O GOD [[*or* LORD]];
let my cry come to you!
² Do not hide your face from me
in the day of my distress!
Incline your ear to me;
answer me speedily in the day when I call!
³ For my days pass away like smoke,
and my bones burn like a furnace.
⁴ My heart is smitten like grass, and withered;
I forget to eat my bread.
⁵ Because of my loud groaning
my bones cleave to my flesh.
⁶ I am like a vulture of the wilderness,
like an owl of the waste places;
⁷ I lie awake,
I am like a lonely bird on the housetop.
⁸ All the day my enemies taunt me,
those who deride me use my name for a curse.
⁹ For I eat ashes like bread,
and mingle tears with my drink,
¹⁰ because of your indignation and anger;
for you have taken me up and thrown me away.
¹¹ My days are like an evening shadow;
I wither away like grass.
¹² But you, O GOD [[*or* LORD]], are enthroned forever;
your name endures to all generations.

PENTECOST 13
YEAR B

Psalm 103:1-13

¹ Bless GOD [[*or* the LORD]], O my soul;
   and all that is within me, bless God's holy name!
² Bless GOD [[*or* the LORD]], O my soul,
   and forget not all God's benefits,
³ who forgives all your iniquity,
   who heals all your diseases,
⁴ who redeems your life from the Pit,
   who crowns you with steadfast love and mercy,
⁵ who satisfies you with good as long as you live
   so that your youth is renewed like the eagle's.
⁶ GOD [[*or* The LORD]] works vindication
   and justice for all who are oppressed.
⁷ God made known God's ways to Moses,
   God's acts to the people of Israel.
⁸ GOD [[*or* The LORD]] is merciful and gracious,
   slow to anger and abounding in steadfast love,
⁹ not always chiding,
   and not remaining angry forever.
¹⁰ God does not deal with us according to our sins,
   nor repay us according to our iniquities.
¹¹ For as the heavens are high above the earth,
   so great is God's steadfast love toward those who fear God;
¹² as far as the east is from the west,
   so far does God remove our transgressions from us.
¹³ As parents* pity their children,
   so GOD [[*or* the LORD]] pities those who fear God.

---

*RSV *a father.* See Appendix, Metaphor.

PENTECOST 9
YEAR A
EPIPHANY 8
YEAR B
LENT 3
YEAR C

Psalm 104:24-34

24 O GOD [[or LORD]], how manifold are your works!
   In wisdom you have made them all;
   the earth is full of your creatures.

Hallelujah!
I will sing to God as long as I live.

25 Yonder is the sea, great and wide,
   which teems with things innumerable,
   living things both small and great.
26 There go the ships,
   and Leviathan which you formed to sport in it.
27 These all look to you,
   to give them their food in due season.

Hallelujah!
I will sing to God as long as I live.

28 When you give to them, they gather it up;
   when you open your hand, they are filled with good things.
29 When you hide your face, they are dismayed;
   when you take away their breath, they die
   and return to their dust.
30 When you send forth your Spirit, they are created;
   and you renew the face of the ground.

Hallelujah!
I will sing to God as long as I live.

31 May the glory of GOD [[or the LORD]] endure forever,
   may GOD [[or the LORD]] rejoice in God's works,
32 who looks on the earth and it trembles,
   who touches the mountains and they smoke!

Hallelujah!
I will sing to God as long as I live.

33 I will sing to GOD [[or the LORD]] as long as I live;
   I will sing praise to my God while I have being.
34 May my meditation be pleasing to God,
   in whom I rejoice.

Hallelujah!
I will sing to God as long as I live.

PENTECOST
YEARS A, B, C

Psalm 105:1-11

1 O give thanks to GOD [[*or* the LORD]], call on God's name,
   make known God's deeds among the nations!
2 Sing to God, sing praises to God,
   tell of all God's wonderful works!
3 Glory in God's holy name;
   let the hearts of those who seek GOD [[*or* the LORD]] rejoice!
4 Seek GOD [[*or* the LORD]] and God's strength,
   seek God's presence continually!
5 Remember the wonderful works that God has done,
   the miracles, and the judgments God uttered,
6 O offspring of Abraham [*and Sarah,**] God's servants,
   children of Jacob, [*Rachel, and Leah,] God's chosen ones!**
7 This is the SOVEREIGN [[*or* LORD]] our God,
   whose judgments are in all the earth.
8 God is mindful of the covenant forever,
   of the word commanded for a thousand generations,
9 the covenant which God made with Abraham,
   God's sworn promise to Isaac,
10 confirmed to Jacob as a statute,
   to Israel as an everlasting covenant,
11 saying, "To you I will give the land of Canaan
   as your portion for an inheritance."

---

*Addition to the text. See "Addition of Women's Names to the Text" in the Appendix.

PENTECOST 10
YEAR A
LENT 2
YEAR B

Psalm 106:4-12, 19-23

4 Remember me, O God [or Lord], when you show favor
to your people;
help me when you deliver them;
5 that I may see the prosperity of your chosen ones,
that I may rejoice in the gladness of your nation,
that I may glory with your heritage.
6 Both we and our ancestors have sinned;
we have committed iniquity, we have done wickedly.
7 Our ancestors, when they were in Egypt,
did not consider your wonderful works;
they did not remember the abundance of your steadfast love,
but rebelled against the Most High at the Red Sea,
8 yet were saved for the sake of God's name,
in order to make known God's mighty power.
9 God rebuked the Red Sea, and it became dry,
and God led them through the deep as through a desert.
10 So God saved them from the hand of the foe,
and delivered them from the power of the enemy.
11 And the waters covered their adversaries;
not one of them was left.
12 Then they believed God's words;
they sang God's praise.
19 They made a calf in Horeb
and worshiped a molten image.
20 They exchanged the glory of God
for the image of an ox that eats grass.
21 They forgot God, their Savior,
who had done great things in Egypt,
22 wondrous works in the land of Ham,
and terrible things by the Red Sea.
23 Therefore God vowed to destroy them—
had not Moses, God's chosen one,
stood in the breach before God,
to turn away God's wrath from destroying them.

PENTECOST 12
YEAR A (Verses 4-12)
PENTECOST 18
YEAR A (Verses 7-8, 19-23)

Psalm 107:1-9, 33-43

¹ O give thanks to God [[*or* the LORD]], for God is good;
God's steadfast love endures forever!
² Let the redeemed of GOD [[*or* the LORD]] say so,
whom God has redeemed from trouble
³ and gathered in from the lands,
from the east and from the west,
from the north and from the south.

O give thanks to God, for God is good.

⁴ Some wandered in desert wastes,
finding no way to a city to dwell in;
⁵ hungry and thirsty,
their soul fainted within them.

O give thanks to God, for God is good.

⁶ Then in their trouble they cried to GOD [[*or* the LORD]],
who delivered them from their distress,
⁷ and led them by a straight way,
till they reached a city to dwell in.

O give thanks to God, for God is good.

⁸ Let them thank GOD [[*or* the LORD]] for God's steadfast love,
for God's wonderful works to humankind!
⁹ For God satisfies the thirsty,
and fills the hungry with good things.

O give thanks to God, for God is good.

³³ God turns rivers into a desert,
springs of water into thirsty ground,
³⁴ a fruitful land into a salty waste,
because of the wickedness of its inhabitants.

O give thanks to God, for God is good.

³⁵ God turns a desert into pools of water,
a parched land into springs of water.
³⁶ And there God lets the hungry dwell,
and they establish a city to live in;
³⁷ they sow fields, and plant vineyards,
and get a fruitful yield.

O give thanks to God, for God is good.

³⁸ They multiply greatly by the blessing of God,
who does not let their cattle decrease.
³⁹ When they are diminished and brought low
through oppression, trouble, and sorrow,
⁴⁰ God pours contempt upon princes
and makes them wander in tractless wastes;
⁴¹ but God raises up those who are needy out of affliction,
and makes their families like flocks.

O give thanks to God, for God is good.

⁴² The upright see it and are glad;
and all wickedness stops its mouth.
⁴³ Whoever is wise should give heed to these things;
let people consider the steadfast love of GOD [[*or* the LORD]].

O give thanks to God, for God is good.

PENTECOST 18
YEAR C (Verses 1-9)
PENTECOST 19
YEAR C (Verses 1, 33–43)

Psalm 111

1 Praise GOD [[*or* the LORD]]!

   **I will give thanks to GOD [[*or* the LORD]] with my whole heart,
   in the company of the upright, in the congregation.**

2 Great are the works of GOD [[*or* the LORD]],

   studied by all who have pleasure in them.

3 Full of honor and majesty is God's work,

   and God's righteousness endures forever.

4 God has caused God's wonderful works to be remembered,
   and is gracious and merciful,

5 **providing food for those who fear God
   and being ever mindful of the covenant.**

6 God has shown God's people the power of God's works,

   in giving them the heritage of the nations.

7 The works of God's hands are faithful and just;

   all God's precepts are trustworthy,

8 they are established forever and ever,

   to be performed with faithfulness and uprightness.

9 God sent redemption to God's people,
   and has commanded the covenant forever.

   Holy and terrible is God's name!

10 The fear of GOD [[*or* the LORD]] is the beginning of wisdom;
   a good understanding have all those who practice it.

   God's praise endures forever!

CHRISTMAS 1
YEARS A, B, C
EPIPHANY 4
YEAR B

104

Psalm 112:4-9

⁴ Light illumines the darkness for the upright;
  GOD [[*or* the LORD]] is gracious, merciful, and righteous.
⁵ It is well with those who deal generously and lend,
  who conduct their affairs with justice.
⁶ For the righteous will never be moved;
  they will be remembered forever.
⁷ They are not afraid of evil tidings;
  their heart is firm, trusting in GOD [[*or* the LORD]].
⁸ Their heart is steady, they will not be afraid,
  until they see their desire on their adversaries.
⁹ They have distributed freely, and have given to the poor;
  their righteousness endures forever;
  their horn is exalted in honor.

Psalm 113

1 Praise GOD [[*or* the LORD]]!
  Praise, O servants of GOD [[*or* the LORD]],
  praise the name of the SOVEREIGN [[*or* LORD]]!
2 Blessed be the name of the SOVEREIGN [[*or* LORD]]
  from this time forth and forevermore!
3 From the rising of the sun to its setting
  the name of the SOVEREIGN [[*or* LORD]] is to be praised!
4 GOD [[*or* The LORD]] is high above all nations,
  and God's glory above the heavens!
5 Who is like the SOVEREIGN [[*or* LORD]] our God,
  who is seated on high,
6 who looks far down
  upon the heavens and the earth?
7 God raises the poor from the dust,
  and lifts the needy from the ash heap,
8 to make them sit with nobles,
  with the nobles of God's people.
9 God gives the barren woman a home,
  making her the joyous mother of children.

Unison:
  Praise GOD [[*or* the LORD]]!

VISITATION—MAY 31
YEARS A, B, C
PENTECOST 3
YEAR C

Psalm 114

1 When Israel went forth from Egypt,
the house of Jacob from a people of strange language,
2 Judah became their sanctuary,
Israel their dominion.
3 The sea looked and fled,
Jordan turned back.
4 The mountains skipped like rams,
the hills like lambs.
5 What ails you, O sea, that you flee?
O Jordan, that you turn back?
6 O mountains, that you skip like rams?
O hills, like lambs?
7 Tremble, O earth, at the presence of GOD [[*or* the LORD]],
at the presence of the God of Jacob,
8 who turns the rock into a pool of water,
the flint into a spring of water.

PENTECOST 15
YEAR A

Psalm 115:1-11

1 Not to us, O GOD [[*or* LORD]], not to us, but to your name give glory,
for the sake of your steadfast love and your faithfulness!

2 Why should the nations say,
"Where is their God?"

3 Our God is in the heavens,
and does whatever God pleases.

4 Their idols are silver and gold,
the work of human hands.

5 They have mouths, but do not speak;
eyes, but do not see.

6 They have ears, but do not hear;
noses, but do not smell.

7 They have hands, but do not feel;
feet, but do not walk;
and they do not make a sound in their throat.

8 Those who make them are like them;
so are all who trust in them.

9 O Israel, trust in GOD [[*or* the LORD]],
who is their help and their shield!

10 O house of Aaron, put your trust in GOD [[*or* the LORD]],
who is their help and their shield!

11 You who fear GOD [[*or* the LORD]], trust in GOD [[*or* the LORD]],
who is their help and their shield!

Psalm 116:1-9, 12-19

(Psalm 116:12-19 is used at the Eucharist on Maundy [Holy] Thursday. Psalm 89:20-21, 24, 26, page 81, is used at the Chrism service.)

1 I love GOD [[*or* the LORD]], because God has heard
my voice and my supplications.

2 **Because God has listened to me,**
therefore I will call on God as long as I live.

3 The snares of death encompassed me;
the pangs of Sheol laid hold on me;
I suffered distress and anguish.

4 Then I called on the name of GOD [[*or* the LORD]]:
"O GOD [[*or* LORD]], I beseech you, save my life!"

5 GOD [[*or* The LORD]] is gracious and righteous;
our God is merciful.

6 GOD [[*or* The LORD]] preserves the simple;
when I was brought low, God saved me.

7 Return, O my soul, to your rest;
for GOD [[*or* the LORD]] has dealt bountifully with you.

8 For you have delivered my soul from death,
my eyes from tears,
my feet from stumbling;

9 I walk before GOD [[*or* the LORD]]
in the land of the living.

12 What shall I render to GOD [[*or* the LORD]]
for all God's bounty to me?

13 **I will lift up the cup of salvation**
and call on the name of GOD [[*or* the LORD]],

14 I will pay my vows to GOD [[*or* the LORD]]
in the presence of all God's people.

15 Precious in the sight of GOD [[*or* the LORD]]
is the death of the saints.

(Continued on page 110)

¹⁶ O God [[*or* Lord]], I am your servant;
I am your servant, the child of your womanservant.
You have loosed my bonds.

¹⁷ I will offer to you the sacrifice of thanksgiving
and call on the name of God [[*or* the Lord]].

¹⁸ I will pay my vows to God [[*or* the Lord]]
in the presence of all God's people,

¹⁹ in the courts of the house of God [[*or* the Lord]],
in your midst, O Jerusalem.

Unison:

Praise God [[*or* the Lord]]!

Lent 5
Year A (Verses 1-9)
Maundy Thursday
Years A, B, C (Verses 12-19)
Easter 3
Year A (Verses 12-19)

Psalm 117

¹ Praise GOD [[*or* the LORD]], all nations!
  Extol God, all people!
² For great is God's steadfast love toward us;
  and the faithfulness of GOD [[*or* the LORD]] endures forever.

Unison:

  Praise GOD [[*or* the LORD]]!

Unison:

¹ **Praise GOD [[*or* the LORD]], all nations!**
  Extol God, all people!
² **For great is God's steadfast love toward us;**
  and the faithfulness of GOD [[*or* the LORD]] endures forever.
  Praise GOD [[*or* the LORD]]!

JANUARY 1 (NEW YEAR)
YEAR A

111

Psalm 118:14-24

¹⁴ GOD [*or* The LORD] is my strength and my song,
  and has become my salvation.
¹⁵ Hark, glad songs of victory
  in the tents of the righteous:
  "The right hand of GOD [*or* the LORD] does valiantly,
¹⁶ the right hand of GOD [*or* the LORD] is exalted,
  the right hand of GOD [*or* the LORD] does valiantly!"

Hallelujah!
This is the day God has made.

¹⁷ I shall not die, but I shall live,
  and recount the deeds of GOD [*or* the LORD].
¹⁸ GOD [*or* The LORD] has chastened me sorely,
  but has not given me over to death.

Hallelujah!
This is the day God has made.

¹⁹ Open to me the gates of righteousness,
  that I may enter through them
  and give thanks to GOD [*or* the LORD].
²⁰ This is the gate of GOD [*or* the LORD];
  the righteous shall enter through it.

Hallelujah!
This is the day God has made.

²¹ I thank you that you have answered me
  and have become my salvation.
²² The stone which the builders rejected
  has become the head of the corner.

Hallelujah!
This is the day God has made.

²³ This is GOD's [*or* the LORD's] doing;
  it is marvelous in our eyes.
²⁴ This is the day which GOD [*or* the LORD] has made;
  let us rejoice and be glad in it.

Hallelujah!
This is the day God has made.

EASTER
YEARS A, B, C (Verses 14-24)

112

Psalm 118:19-29

¹⁹ Open to me the gates of righteousness,
   that I may enter through them
   and give thanks to GOD ⟦*or* the LORD⟧.

O give thanks to God, for God is good.

²⁰ This is the gate of GOD ⟦*or* the LORD⟧;
   the righteous shall enter through it.
²¹ I thank you that you have answered me
   and have become my salvation.

O give thanks to God, for God is good.

²² The stone which the builders rejected
   has become the head of the corner.
²³ This is GOD's ⟦*or* the LORD's⟧ doing;
   it is marvelous in our eyes.
²⁴ This is the day which GOD ⟦*or* the LORD⟧ has made;
   let us rejoice and be glad in it.

O give thanks to God, for God is good.

²⁵ Save us, we beseech you, O GOD ⟦*or* LORD⟧!
   O GOD ⟦*or* LORD⟧, we beseech you, give us success!
²⁶ Blessed be the one who enters in the name of GOD ⟦*or* the LORD⟧!
   We bless you from the house of GOD ⟦*or* the LORD⟧.

O give thanks to God, for God is good.

²⁷ The SOVEREIGN ⟦*or* LORD⟧ is God,
   who has caused light to shine upon us.
   Bind the festal procession with branches,
   up to the horns of the altar!

O give thanks to God, for God is good.

²⁸ You are my God, and I will give thanks to you;
   you are my God, I will extol you.
²⁹ O give thanks to GOD ⟦*or* the LORD⟧, for God is good;
   for God's steadfast love endures forever!

O give thanks to God, for God is good.

LENT 6, PALM SUNDAY
YEARS A, B, C (Verses 19-29)

Psalm 119:1-8

1 Blessed are those whose way is blameless,
  who walk in the law of GOD [[*or* the LORD]]!

2 Blessed are those who keep God's testimonies,
  who seek God with their whole heart,

3 who also do no wrong,
  but walk in God's ways!

4 You have commanded your precepts to be kept diligently.

5 **O that my ways may be steadfast**
  in keeping your statutes!

6 Then I shall not be put to shame,
  having my eyes fixed on all your commandments.

7 I will praise you with an upright heart,
  when I learn your righteous ordinances.

8 I will observe your statutes;
  O forsake me not completely!

Psalm 119:33-48

³³ Teach me, O GOD [[*or* LORD]], the way of your statutes;
 and I will keep it to the end.
³⁴ Give me understanding, that I may keep your law
 and observe it with my whole heart.
³⁵ Lead me in the path of your commandments,
 for I delight in it.
³⁶ Incline my heart to your testimonies,
 and not to gain!
³⁷ Turn my eyes from looking at vanities;
 and give me life in your ways.
³⁸ Confirm to your servant your promise,
 which is for those who fear you.
³⁹ Turn away the reproach which I dread;
 for your ordinances are good.
⁴⁰ I long for your precepts;
 in your righteousness give me life!
⁴¹ Let your steadfast love come to me, O GOD [[*or* LORD]],
 your salvation according to your promise;
⁴² then I shall have an answer for those who taunt me,
 for I trust in your word.
⁴³ And take not the word of truth utterly out of my mouth,
 for my hope is in your ordinances.
⁴⁴ I will keep your law continually,
 forever and ever;
⁴⁵ and I shall walk at liberty,
 for I have sought your precepts.
⁴⁶ I will also speak of your testimonies before rulers,⬜
 and shall not be put to shame;
⁴⁷ for I find my delight in your commandments,
 which I love.
⁴⁸ I revere your commandments, which I love,
 and I will meditate on your statutes.

⬜RSV *kings*. See Appendix.

EPIPHANY 8
YEAR A (Verses 33-40)
PENTECOST 24
YEAR B (Verses 33-48)

Psalm 119:129-136

129 Your testimonies are wonderful;
   therefore my soul keeps them.
130 The unfolding of your words gives light;
   it imparts understanding to those who are simple.
131 With open mouth I pant,
   because I long for your commandments.
132 Turn to me and be gracious to me,
   as is your wont toward those who love your name.
133 Keep steady my steps according to your promise,
   and let no iniquity get dominion over me.
134 Redeem me from human oppression,
   that I may keep your precepts.
135 Make your face shine upon your servant,
   and teach me your statutes.
136 My eyes shed streams of tears,
   because people do not keep your law.

Psalm 119:137-144

¹³⁷ Righteous are you, O GOD [[*or* LORD]],
   and right are your judgments.
¹³⁸ You have appointed your testimonies in righteousness
   and in all faithfulness.
¹³⁹ My zeal consumes me,
   because my foes forget your words.
¹⁴⁰ Your promise is well tried,
   and your servant loves it.
¹⁴¹ I am small and despised,
   yet I do not forget your precepts.
¹⁴² Your righteousness is righteous forever,
   and your law is true.
¹⁴³ Trouble and anguish have come upon me,
   but your commandments are my delight.
¹⁴⁴ Your testimonies are righteous forever;
   give me understanding that I may live.

Psalm 121

¹ I lift up my eyes to the hills.
  From whence does my help come?

² My help comes from GOD [[*or* the LORD]],
  who made heaven and earth.

³ God will not let your foot be moved;
  the one who keeps you will not slumber;

⁴ the one who keeps Israel
  will neither slumber nor sleep.

⁵ GOD [[*or* The LORD]] is your keeper;
  **GOD [[*or* the LORD]] is your shade
  on your right hand.**

⁶ The sun shall not smite you by day,
  nor the moon by night.

⁷ GOD [[*or* The LORD]] will keep you from all evil,
  and will keep your life.

⁸ GOD [[*or* The LORD]] will keep
  your going out and your coming in
  from this time forth and forevermore.

Psalm 122

¹ I was glad when they said to me,
  "Let us go to the house of God ⟦*or* the Lord⟧!"
² Our feet have been standing
  within your gates, O Jerusalem!
³ Jerusalem, built as a city
  which is bound firmly together,
⁴ to which the tribes go up,
  the tribes of God ⟦*or* the Lord⟧,
  **as was decreed for Israel,
  to give thanks to the name of God ⟦*or* the Lord⟧.**
⁵ There thrones for judgment were set,
  the thrones of the house of David.
⁶ Pray for the peace of Jerusalem!
  "May they prosper who love you!
⁷ Peace be within your walls,
  and security within your towers!"
⁸ For the sake of my kin and companions
  I will say, "Peace be within you!"
⁹ For the sake of the house of the Sovereign ⟦*or* Lord⟧ our God,
  I will seek your good.

Psalm 124

1 If it had not been GOD [[*or* the LORD]] who was on our side,
let Israel now say—

2 **if it had not been GOD [[*or* the LORD]] who was on our side,**
when people rose up against us,

3 then they would have swallowed us up alive,

when their anger was kindled against us;

4 then the flood would have swept us away,

the torrent would have gone over us;

5 then over us would have gone
the raging waters.

6 **Blessed be GOD [[*or* the LORD]],**
who has not given us
as prey to their teeth!

7 We have escaped as a bird
from the snare of the fowlers;

the snare is broken,
and we have escaped!

8 Our help is in the name of GOD [[*or* the LORD]],

who made heaven and earth.

Psalm 125

¹ Those who trust in GOD [[*or* the LORD]] are like Mount Zion,
which cannot be moved, but abides forever.

² As the mountains are round about Jerusalem,
so GOD [[*or* the LORD]] is round about God's people,
from this time forth and forevermore.

³ For the scepter of wickedness shall not rest
upon the land allotted to the righteous,
lest the righteous put forth
their hands to do wrong.

⁴ Do good, O GOD [[*or* LORD]], to those who are good,
and to those who are upright in their hearts!

⁵ But those who turn aside upon their crooked ways
GOD [[*or* the LORD]] **will lead away with evildoers!**

Unison:

Peace be in Israel!

Psalm 126

1 When GOD [[*or* the LORD]] restored the fortunes of Zion,
  we were like those who dream.
2 Then our mouth was filled with laughter,
  and our tongue with shouts of joy;
  then they said among the nations,
  "GOD [[*or* The LORD]] has done great things for them."
3 GOD [[*or* The LORD]] has done great things for us;
  we are glad.
4 Restore our fortunes, O GOD [[*or* LORD]],
  like the watercourses in the Negeb!
5 May those who sow in tears
  reap with shouts of joy!
6 Those who go forth weeping,
  bearing the seed for sowing,
  shall come home with shouts of joy,
  bringing their sheaves of grain.

PENTECOST 23
YEAR B
THANKSGIVING DAY
YEAR B
ADVENT 2
YEAR C
LENT 5
YEAR C

Psalm 127

¹ Unless GOD [[*or* the LORD]] builds the house,
those who build it labor in vain.
Unless GOD [[*or* the LORD]] watches over the city,
the watcher stays awake in vain.
² It is in vain that you rise up early
and go late to rest,
eating the bread of anxious toil;
for God gives sleep to God's beloved.
³ Children are a heritage from GOD [[*or* the LORD]],
the fruit of the womb a reward.
⁴ Like arrows in the hand of a warrior
are the children of one's youth.
⁵ Happy is the one who has
a quiver full of them!
That one shall not be put to shame
when speaking with enemies in the gate.

PENTECOST 24
YEAR A
LENT 2
YEAR C

Psalm 128

¹ Blessed is everyone who fears God [[*or* the Lord]],
who walks in God's ways!

² You shall eat the fruit of the labor of your hands;
you shall be happy, and it shall be well with you.

³ Your beloved will be like a fruitful vine
within your house;
**your children will be like olive shoots
around your table.**

⁴ Thus shall the one be blessed
who fears God [[*or* the Lord]].

⁵ God [[*or* The Lord]] bless you from Zion!
**May you see the prosperity of Jerusalem
all the days of your life!**

⁶ May you see your children's children!
Peace be upon Israel!

Pentecost 23
Year A
Pentecost 20
Year B

Psalm 130

¹ Out of the depths I cry to you, O GOD [[*or* LORD]]!

² **God [[*or* Lord]], hear my voice!**
Let your ears be attentive
to the voice of my supplications!

³ If you, O GOD [[*or* LORD]], should mark iniquities,
God [[*or* Lord]], who could stand?

⁴ But there is forgiveness with you,
that you may be feared.

⁵ I wait for GOD [[*or* the LORD]], my soul waits,
and in God's word I hope;

⁶ my soul waits for GOD [[*or* the LORD]]
more than those who watch for the morning,
more than those who watch for the morning.

⁷ O Israel, hope in GOD [[*or* the LORD]]!
**For with GOD [[*or* the LORD]] there is steadfast love,
and with God is plenteous redemption.**

⁸ And God will redeem Israel
from all their iniquities.

Psalm 132:11-18

¹¹ GOD [[*or* The LORD]] swore to David a sure oath
and will not turn back from it:

**"One from the fruit of your body
I will set on your throne.**

¹² If your children keep my covenant
and my testimonies which I shall teach them,

**their children also forever
shall sit upon your throne."**

¹³ For GOD [[*or* the LORD]] has chosen Zion,

and has desired it for a habitation:

¹⁴ "This is my resting place forever;

here I will dwell, for I have desired it.

¹⁵ I will abundantly bless its provisions;

I will satisfy its poor with bread.

¹⁶ Its priests I will clothe with salvation,

and its saints will shout for joy.

¹⁷ There I will make a horn to sprout for David;

I have prepared a lamp for my anointed,

¹⁸ whose enemies I will clothe with shame;

but upon my anointed the crown will shed its luster."

Psalm 133

¹ How good and pleasant it is
when brothers and sisters dwell in unity!

² It is like fragrant oil upon the head,
running down upon the face,

upon the face of Aaron,
running down on the collar of the robes!

³ It is like the dew of Hermon,
which falls on the mountains of Zion!

For there GOD [*or* the LORD] **has commanded the blessing,**
life forevermore.

Unison:

¹ **How good and pleasant it is**
when brothers and sisters dwell in unity!

² **It is like fragrant oil upon the head,**
running down upon the face,
upon the face of Aaron,
running down on the collar of the robes!

³ **It is like the dew of Hermon,**
which falls on the mountains of Zion!
For there GOD [*or* the LORD] **has commanded the blessing,**
life forevermore.

Psalm 135:1-14

1 Praise GOD [[*or* the LORD]].
Praise the name of GOD [[*or* the LORD]],
give praise, O servants of GOD [[*or* the LORD]],
2 you that stand in the house of GOD [[*or* the LORD]],
in the courts of the house of our God!
3 Praise GOD [[*or* the LORD]], for GOD [[*or* the LORD]] is good;
sing to God's name, for God is gracious!
4 For GOD [[*or* the LORD]] has chosen Jacob for Godself,
Israel as God's own possession.
5 For I know that GOD [[*or* the LORD]] is great,
and that our God [[*or* Lord]] is above all gods.
6 Whatever GOD [[*or* the LORD]] pleases God does,
in heaven and on earth,
in the seas and all deeps.
7 God it is who makes the clouds rise at the end of the earth,
who makes lightnings for the rain
and brings forth the wind from God's storehouses.
8 God it was who smote the firstborn of Egypt,
both human and animal;
9 who in your midst, O Egypt,
sent signs and wonders
against Pharaoh and all his servants;
10 who smote many nations
and slew mighty kings,
11 Sihon, king of the Amorites,
and Og, king of Bashan,
and all the kingdoms of Canaan,
12 and gave their land as a heritage,
a heritage to God's people Israel.
13 Your name, O GOD [[*or* LORD]], endures forever,
your renown, O GOD [[*or* LORD]], throughout all ages.
14 For GOD [[*or* the LORD]] will vindicate God's people,
and have compassion on God's servants.

PENTECOST 21
YEAR A

128

Psalm 137:1-6

1 By the waters of Babylon,

there we sat down and wept,
when we remembered Zion.

2 On the willows there

we hung up our lyres.

3 For there our captors
required of us songs,
and our tormentors, mirth, saying,

"Sing us one of the songs of Zion!"

4 How shall we sing GOD'S [[*or* the LORD'S]] song
in a foreign land?

5 **If I forget you, O Jerusalem,**
let my right hand wither!

6 Let my tongue cleave to the roof of my mouth,
if I do not remember you,

if I do not set Jerusalem
above my highest joy!

LENT 4
YEAR B

Psalm 138

¹ I give you thanks, O GOD [[*or* LORD]], with my whole heart;
  before the gods I sing your praise;
² I bow down toward your holy temple
  and give thanks to your name for your steadfast love
  and your faithfulness;
  for you have exalted above everything
  your name and your word.
³ On the day I called you, you answered me,
  my strength of soul you increased.
⁴ All the rulers□ of the earth shall praise you, O GOD [[*or* LORD]],
  for they have heard the words of your mouth;
⁵ and they shall sing of the ways of GOD [[*or* the LORD]],
  for great is the glory of GOD [[*or* the LORD]].
⁶ For GOD [[*or* the LORD]], though high, regards the lowly,
  but knows the haughty from afar.
⁷ Though I walk in the midst of trouble,
  you preserve my life;
  you stretch out your hand against the wrath of my enemies,
  and your right hand delivers me.
⁸ GOD's [[*or* The LORD's]] purpose for me will be fulfilled;
  your steadfast love, O GOD [[*or* LORD]], endures forever.

Unison:

Do not forsake the work of your hands.

□RSV *kings.* See Appendix.

Psalm 139:1-18

1 O GOD [*or* LORD], you have searched me and known me!
2 You know when I sit down and when I rise up;

   you discern my thoughts from afar.

3 You search out my path and my lying down,

   and are acquainted with all my ways.

4 Even before a word is on my tongue,

   O GOD [*or* LORD], you know it altogether.

5 You beset me behind and before,

   and lay your hand upon me.

6 Such knowledge is too wonderful for me;

   it is high, I cannot attain it.

7 Where shall I go from your Spirit?

   Or where shall I flee from your presence?

8 If I ascend to heaven, you are there!

   If I make my bed in Sheol, you are there!

9 If I take the wings of the morning
   and dwell in the uttermost parts of the sea,

10 **even there your hand shall lead me,**
   and your right hand shall hold me.

11 If I say, "Let only darkness cover me,

   and the light about me be night,"

12 even the darkness is not dark to you,
   the night is bright as the day;

   for darkness is as light with you.

13 For you formed my inward parts,

   you knit me together in my mother's womb.

14 I praise you, for you are fearful and wonderful.

   Wonderful are your works!

   You know me right well;
15 my frame was not hidden from you,

   when I was being made in secret,
   intricately wrought in the depths of the earth.

(Continued on page 132)

¹⁶ Your eyes beheld my unformed substance;
  in your book were written, every one of them,
  the days that were formed for me,
  when as yet there was none of them.
¹⁷ How precious to me are your thoughts, O God!
  How vast is the sum of them!
¹⁸ If I would count them, they are more than the sand.
  When I awake, I am still with you.

PENTECOST 8
YEAR C (Verses 1-12)
PENTECOST 9
YEAR C (Verses 13-18)

Psalm 143:1-10

1 Hear my prayer, O God [[*or* Lord]]; give ear to my supplications!
In your faithfulness answer me, in your righteousness!

2 Enter not into judgment with your servant;
for no one living is righteous before you.

3 For the enemy has pursued me,
has crushed my life to the ground,
and has made me sit in darkness like those long dead.

4 Therefore my spirit faints within me;
my heart within me is appalled.

5 I remember the days of old,
I meditate on all that you have done;
I muse on what your hands have wrought.

6 I stretch out my hands to you;
my soul thirsts for you like a parched land.

7 Make haste to answer me, O God [[*or* Lord]]!
My spirit fails!
Hide not your face from me,
lest I be like those who go down to the Pit.

8 Let me hear in the morning of your steadfast love,
for in you I put my trust.
Teach me the way I should go,
for to you I lift up my soul.

9 Deliver me, O God [[*or* Lord]], from my enemies!
I have fled to you for refuge!

10 Teach me to do your will,
for you are my God!
**Let your good spirit lead me
on a level path!**

Pentecost 11
Year A (Verses 1-10)
Pentecost 12
Year B (Verses 1-8)

8 GOD [[or The LORD]] is gracious and merciful,
 slow to anger and abounding in steadfast love.

9 GOD [[or The LORD]] is good to all,
 and has compassion over all that God has made.

10 All your works shall give thanks to you, O GOD [[or LORD]],
 and all your saints shall bless you!

11 They shall speak of the glory of your realm,☆
 and tell of your power,

12 to make known to humankind your mighty deeds,
 and the glorious splendor of your realm.☆

13 Your realm☆ is an everlasting realm,☆
 and your dominion endures throughout all generations.
 GOD [[or The LORD]] is faithful in every word,
 and gracious in every deed.

14 GOD [[or The LORD]] upholds all who are falling,
 and raises up all who are bowed down.

15 The eyes of all look to you,
 and you give them their food in due season.

16 You open your hand,
 and satisfy the desire of every living thing.

17 GOD [[or The LORD]] is just in all God's ways,
 and kind in every act.

18 GOD [[or The LORD]] is near to all who call upon God,
 to all who call upon God in truth.

19 God fulfills the desire of all who fear God,
 and hears their cry, and saves them.

☆RSV *kingdom.* See Appendix.

²⁰ GOD [*or* The LORD] preserves all who love God,
   but will destroy all the wicked.
²¹ My mouth will speak the praise of GOD [*or* the LORD],
   and let all flesh bless God's holy name forever and ever.

Psalm 146

¹ Praise GOD [[*or* the LORD]]!
  Praise GOD [[*or* the LORD]], O my soul!
² I will praise GOD [[*or* the LORD]] as long as I live;
  I will sing praises to my God while I have being.
³ Put not your trust in rulers,
  in mortals, in whom there is no help.
⁴ When their breath departs they return to their earth;
  on that very day their plans perish.
⁵ Happy is the one whose help is the God of Jacob,
  whose hope is in God, the SOVEREIGN [[*or* LORD]],
⁶ who made heaven and earth,
  the sea, and all that is in them;
  who keeps faith forever;
⁷ who executes justice for the oppressed;
  who gives food to the hungry.
  GOD [[*or* The LORD]] sets the prisoners free;
⁸ **GOD [[*or* the LORD]] opens the eyes of those who are blind.**
  GOD [[*or* The LORD]] lifts up those who are bowed down;
  GOD [[*or* the LORD]] loves the righteous.
⁹ GOD [[*or* The LORD]] watches over the sojourners,
  and upholds the widow and the orphan,
  but brings the way of the wicked to ruin.
¹⁰ GOD [[*or* The LORD]] will reign forever,
  your God, O Zion, to all generations.

Unison:
  Praise GOD [[*or* the LORD]]!

ADVENT 3
YEAR A (Verses 5-10)
PENTECOST 22
YEAR A
PENTECOST 25
YEAR B

136

Psalm 147

1 Praise GOD [[or the LORD]]!
 For it is good to sing praises to our God;
  for God is gracious, and a song of praise is seemly.

2 GOD [[or The LORD]] builds up Jerusalem,
  and gathers the outcasts of Israel,

3 heals the brokenhearted,
  and binds up their wounds,

4 determines the number of the stars,
  and gives to all of them their names.

5 Great is our GOD [[or LORD]], and abundant in power,
  with understanding beyond measure.

6 GOD [[or The LORD]] lifts up the downtrodden,
  and casts the wicked to the ground.

7 Sing to GOD [[or the LORD]] with thanksgiving;
  make melody upon the lyre to our God,

8 who covers the heavens with clouds,
 prepares rain for the earth,
  and makes grass grow upon the hills,

9 who gives to the beasts their food,
  and to the young ravens which cry!

10 God does not delight in the strength of the horse,
  nor take pleasure in the might of a human being;

11 but GOD [[or the LORD]] takes pleasure in those who fear God,
  in those who hope in God's steadfast love.

12 Praise GOD [[or the LORD]], O Jerusalem!
  Praise your God, O Zion,

13 for God strengthens the bars of your gates,
  and blesses your children within you,

14 making peace in your borders,
  and filling you with the finest of the wheat.

15 God sends forth a command to the earth;
  God's word runs swiftly.

(Continued on page 138)

¹⁶ God gives snow like wool,
   scattering hoarfrost like ashes,
¹⁷ and casting forth ice like morsels;
   who can stand before God's cold?
¹⁸ God sends forth God's word, and melts them,
   making the wind blow, and the waters flow.
¹⁹ God declares God's word to Jacob,
   God's statutes and ordinances to Israel.
²⁰ God has not dealt thus with any other nation;
   they do not know the ordinances.

Unison:
   Praise GOD [[*or* the LORD]]!

CHRISTMAS 2
YEARS A, B, C (Verses 12-20)
EPIPHANY 5
YEAR B (Verses 1-11)

Psalm 149

1 Praise GOD [[*or* the LORD]]!
  Sing to GOD [[*or* the LORD]] a new song,
  God's praise in the assembly of the faithful!
2 Let Israel be glad in its Maker,
  let the children of Zion rejoice in their Ruler![1]
3 Let them praise God's name with dancing,
  making melody with timbrel and lyre!
4 For GOD [[*or* the LORD]] takes pleasure in God's people,
  and adorns the humble with victory.
5 Let the faithful exult in glory;
  let them sing for joy on their couches.
6 Let the high praises of God be in their throats
  and two-edged swords in their hands,
7 to wreak vengeance on the nations
  and chastisement on the peoples,
8 to bind their rulers[1] with chains
  and their nobles with fetters of iron,
9 to execute on them the judgment written!
  This is glory for all God's faithful ones.

Unison:
  Praise GOD [[*or* the LORD]]!

---

[1]RSV v. 2 *King;* v. 8 *kings.* See Appendix.

ALL SAINTS—NOVEMBER 1
YEAR C

139

Psalm 150

1 Praise GOD [[or the LORD]]!
Praise God in the sanctuary;
praise God in the mighty firmament!
2 Praise God for mighty deeds;
praise God according to God's exceeding greatness!
3 Praise God with trumpet sound;
praise God with lute and harp!
4 Praise God with timbrel and dance;
praise God with strings and pipe!
5 Praise God with sounding cymbals;
praise God with loud clashing cymbals!
6 Let everything that breathes praise GOD [[or the LORD]]!
Praise GOD [[or the LORD]]!

Unison:

1 Praise GOD [[or the LORD]]!
Praise God in the sanctuary;
praise God in the mighty firmament!
2 Praise God for mighty deeds;
praise God according to God's exceeding greatness!
3 Praise God with trumpet sound;
praise God with lute and harp!
4 Praise God with timbrel and dance;
praise God with strings and pipe!
5 Praise God with sounding cymbals;
praise God with loud clashing cymbals!
6 Let everything that breathes praise GOD [[or the LORD]]!
Praise GOD [[or the LORD]]!

EASTER EVENING
YEARS A, B, C

Appendix

Metaphor

A metaphor is a figure of speech used to extend meaning through comparison of dissimilars. For example, "Life is a dream" is a metaphor. The character of dreams is ascribed to life, and the meaning of "life" is thus extended. "Dream" is used as a screen through which to view "life." Two dissimilars are juxtaposed.

The statement "God is Father" is also a metaphor. Two dissimilars, "Father" and "God," are juxtaposed, and so the meaning of "God" is extended. Although "God the Father" has been a powerful metaphor for communicating the nature of God, like any metaphor it can become worn. It may even be interpreted literally, that is, as describing exactly. The dissimilars become similar. The metaphor becomes a proposition. In this psalm book, God is sometimes referred to as "Parent."

Sovereign; God, the SOVEREIGN; etc. (RSV Lord, LORD, etc.)

Sometime in the course of Israel's history the personal name of God, probably pronounced *Yahweh,* ceased to be spoken aloud for fear that it would be profaned, even though it continued to be written in the text of the scriptures. Thus, the practice was already established according to which the faith and piety of the community, shaped by the tradition of scripture itself, takes precedence over the written word in determining what is read for the divine name by the worshiping community. From that time on, the chief word read in place of the divine name was *Adonai*—an honorific title translated "Lord" or "my Lord."

In those places in the RSV where the underlying Hebrew text contains the divine name *(Yahweh),* and not simply the word *Adonai,* the typography is changed to LORD. Where the divine name is found in the original text, the editorial committee prefers to render it as "GOD" or "the SOVEREIGN." However, because of the deep commitment in the church to the word "Lord" in both Old and New Testaments, and because of a certain ambiguity about the extent to which "Lord" is heard as gender-specific, that term has been included in this psalm book as an optional or alternative reading, set off in this manner: [or Lord]; [or LORD].

In this psalm book the Hebrew word *Elohim* is rendered "God," as in the RSV. The word "God" is also usually used for masculine pronouns referring to the "Sovereign [or Lord]" or to "God."

Occasionally the divine name, Yahweh, is found in combination with the word for God *(Yahweh Elohim)* or with the word for Lord *(Adonai Yahweh).* These are rendered in the RSV as "the LORD God" and "the Lord GOD," respectively. In this psalm book the former is rendered as "the SOVEREIGN [or LORD] God" and the latter as "the Sovereign [or Lord] GOD." The following chart summarizes these various renderings.

Hebrew Scriptures	RSV	Inclusive-Language
Elohim	God	God
Adonai	Lord	GOD [[*or* the LORD]]; or the SOVEREIGN [[*or* Lord]]
Yahweh	LORD	GOD [[*or* the LORD]]; or the SOVEREIGN [[*or* LORD]]
Yahweh Elohim; or *Elohim Yahweh*	the LORD God	the SOVEREIGN [[*or* LORD]] God
Adonai Yahweh; or *Yahweh Adonai*	the Lord GOD	the Sovereign [[*or* Lord]] GOD

(✩)Realm (RSV Kingdom)

The Hebrew root usually translated "kingdom" in the RSV is rendered as "realm" in this psalm book.

(▢)Ruler, Monarch (RSV King)

The word "king" is used in the Bible both in reference to earthly royal figures and as a metaphor for God. In this psalm book "King" as a metaphor for God, or in reference to one who rules for God, is rendered as "Ruler," "Sovereign," or occasionally "Monarch." The word "king" is retained in reference to earthly kings, such as David.

(*)Addition of Women's Names to the Text

In a few instances, women's names have been added to the text in this psalm book. These names are included where generation or origin of the people is a major concern. The addition of these names is also consistent with the biblical tradition itself, where on occasion Sarah as well as Abraham is explicitly referred to as progenitor (cf. Isa. 51:1–2). Women's names added to the text are placed in brackets and italicized. If the additional words involve a change in the verb form, the RSV rendering is in the footnotes.

Use of "They," "Them," "Themselves," "Their" as Singular Pronouns

In some cases, indefinite singular pronouns are rendered in this psalm book by "they," "them," "themselves," or "their." This usage is recognized as appropriate by the National Council of Teachers of English in its *Guidelines for Nonsexist Use of Language in NCTE Publications.* The *Oxford English Dictionary* says that "they" is "often used in reference to a singular noun made universal by *every, any,* or *no,* etc., or is applied to one of either sex (= 'he or she')." Those grammarians who oppose this usage follow common practice established by an 1850 Act of Parliament declaring that "he" is generic and legally includes "she." That declaration in turn was based on a rule invented in 1746 by John Kirby: the male gender is "more comprehensive" than the female. This lectionary follows the precedent of St. John Fisher (1535), who wrote that God "never forsaketh any creature unlesse they before have forsaken themselves," and William Shakespeare, who urged "everyone to rest themselves."

Index of Psalms by Sundays and Special Days

Day	Year A	Year B	Year C
Advent 1	122	80:1-7	25:1-10
Advent 2	72:1-8	85:8-13	126
Advent 3	146:5-10	—	—
Advent 4	24	89:1-4, 19-24	80:1-7
Christmas Eve/Day	96	96	96
Christmas Day, Additional, Set 1	97	97	97
Christmas Day, Additional, Set 2	98	98	98
Christmas 1 (or Epiphany)	111	111	111
January 1 (New Year)	117	8	90:1-12
January 1 Holy Name; Solemnity of Mary	67	67	67
Christmas 2	147:12-20	147:12-20	147:12-20
Epiphany	72:1-14	72:1-14	72:1-14
Baptism of Jesus	29	29	29
Epiphany 2	40:1-10	63:1-8	36:5-10
Epiphany 3	27:1-6	62:5-12	19:7-14
Epiphany 4	37:1-11	111	71:1-6
Epiphany 5	112:4-9	147:1-11	138
Epiphany 6	119:1-8	32	1
Epiphany 7	62:5-12	41	37:1-11
Epiphany 8	119:33-40	103:1-13	92:1-4, 12-15
Last Sunday After Epiphany	2:6-11	50:1-6	99
Ash Wednesday	51:1-12	51:1-12	51:1-12
Lent 1	130	25:1-10	91:9-16
Lent 2	33:18-22	105:1-11	127
Lent 3	95	19:7-14	103:1-13
Lent 4	23	137:1-6	34:1-8
Lent 5	116:1-9	51:10-17	126
Lent 6, Passion Sunday	31:9-16	31:9-16	31:9-16
Lent 6, Palm Sunday	118:19-29	118:19-29	118:19-29

Index of Psalms by Sundays and Special Days

Day (cont'd)	Year A (cont'd)	Year B (cont'd)	Year C (cont'd)
Monday of Holy Week	36:5-10	36:5-10	36:5-10
Tuesday of Holy Week	71:1-12	71:1-12	71:1-12
Wednesday of Holy Week	70	70	70
Maundy Thursday	116:12-19	116:12-19	116:12-19
Maundy Thursday, Chrism service	89:20-21, 24, 26	89:20-21, 24, 26	89:20-21, 24, 26
Good Friday	22:1-18	22:1-18	22:1-18
Easter	118:14-24	118:14-24	118:14-24
Easter Evening	150	150	150
Easter 2	16:5-11	133	2
Easter 3	116:12-19	4	30:4-12
Easter 4	23	23	23
Easter 5	31:1-8	22:25-31	145:13b-21
Easter 6	66:8-20	98	67
Ascension	47	47	47
Easter 7	68:1-10	1	97
Pentecost	104:24-34	104:24-34	104:24-34
Trinity	33:1-12	29	8
Pentecost 2	33:12-22	20	100
Pentecost 3	13	57	113
Pentecost 4	46	46	42
Pentecost 5	91:1-10	48	43
Pentecost 6	17:1-7, 15	24	44:1-8
Pentecost 7	124	89:20-37	5:1-8
Pentecost 8	69:6-15	132:11-18	139:1-12
Pentecost 9	103:1-13	53	139:13-18
Pentecost 10	105:1-11	32	21:1-7
Pentecost 11	143:1-10	34:11-22	28
Pentecost 12	106:4-12	143:1-8	14
Pentecost 13	78:1-3, 10-20	102:1-12	10:12-18
Pentecost 14	95	67	84
Pentecost 15	114	121	15

Index of Psalms by Sundays and Special Days

Day (cont'd)	Year A (cont'd)	Year B (cont'd)	Year C (cont'd)
Pentecost 16	115:1-11	119:129-136	94:12-22
Pentecost 17	19:7-14	125	77:11-20
Pentecost 18	106:7-8, 19-23	27:1-6	107:1-9
Pentecost 19	99	27:7-14	107:1, 33-43
Pentecost 20	81:1-10	128	101
Pentecost 21	135:1-14	90:1-12	26
Pentecost 22	146	35:17-28	119:137-144
Pentecost 23	128	126	3
Pentecost 24	127	119:33-48	65:1-8
Pentecost 25	50:7-15	146	9:11-20
Pentecost 26	76	145:8-13a	82
Pentecost 27	23	93	95
Presentation—February 2	84	84	84
Presentation—February 2 (alternate)	24:7-10	24:7-10	24:7-10
Annunciation—March 25	40:6-10	40:6-10	40:6-10
Visitation—May 31	113	113	113
Holy Cross—September 14	98:1-5	98:1-5	98:1-5
Holy Cross—September 14 (alternate)	78:1-2, 34-38	78:1-2, 34-38	78:1-2, 34-38
All Saints—November 1	34:1-10	24:1-6	149
Thanksgiving Day	65	126	100

Index of Psalms for Church Years

Psalm	Year A	Year B	Year C
1		Easter 7	Epiphany 6
2			Easter 2
2:6-11	Epiphany 9		
3			Pentecost 23
4		Easter 3	
5:1-8			Pentecost 7
8		January 1 (New Year)	Trinity
9:11-20			Pentecost 25
10:12-18			Pentecost 13
13	Pentecost 3		
14			Pentecost 12
15			Pentecost 15
16:5-11	Easter 2		
17:1-7, 15	Pentecost 6		
19:7-14	Pentecost 17	Lent 3	Epiphany 3
20		Pentecost 2	
21:1-7			Pentecost 10
22:1-18	Good Friday	Good Friday	Good Friday
22:25-31		Easter 5	
23	Lent 4	Easter 4	Easter 4
	Easter 4		
	Pentecost 27		
24	Advent 4	Pentecost 6	
24:1-6		All Saints—November 1	
24:7-10	Presentation—Feb. 2 (alternate)	Presentation (alternate)	Presentation (alternate)
25:1-10		Lent 1	Advent 1
26			Pentecost 21
27:1-6	Epiphany 3	Pentecost 18	
27:7-14		Pentecost 19	
28			Pentecost 11
29	Baptism of Jesus	Baptism of Jesus	Baptism of Jesus
		Trinity	

Index of Psalms for Church Years

Psalm (cont'd)	Year A (cont'd)	Year B (cont'd)	Year C (cont'd)
30:4-12			Easter 3
31:1-8	Easter 5		
31:9-16	Lent 6, Passion Sunday	Lent 6, Passion Sunday	Lent 6, Passion Sunday
32		Epiphany 6 Pentecost 10	
33:1-12	Trinity		
33:12-22	Pentecost 2		
33:18-22	Lent 2		
34:1-8			Lent 4
34:1-10	All Saints— November 1		
34:11-22		Pentecost 11	
35:17-28		Pentecost 22	
36:5-10	Monday of Holy Week	Monday of Holy Week	Epiphany 2 Monday of Holy Week
37:1-11	Epiphany 4		Epiphany 7
40:1-10	Epiphany 2		
40:6-10	Annunciation— March 25	Annunciation	Annunciation
41		Epiphany 7	
42			Pentecost 4
43			Pentecost 5
44:1-8			Pentecost 6
46	Pentecost 4	Pentecost 4	
47	Ascension	Ascension	Ascension
48		Pentecost 5	
50:1-6		Last Sunday After Epiphany	
50:7-15	Pentecost 25		
51:1-12	Ash Wednesday	Ash Wednesday	Ash Wednesday
51:10-17		Lent 5	
53		Pentecost 9	
57		Pentecost 3	

148

Index of Psalms for Church Years

Psalm (cont'd)	Year A (cont'd)	Year B (cont'd)	Year C (cont'd)
62:5-12	Epiphany 7	Epiphany 3	
63:1-8		Epiphany 2	
65	Thanksgiving Day		
65:1-8			Pentecost 24
66:8-20	Easter 6		
67	January 1 Holy Name; Solemnity of Mary	January 1 Holy Name; Solemnity of Mary	January 1 Holy Name; Solemnity of Mary
		Pentecost 14	Easter 6
68:1-10	Easter 7		
69:6-15	Pentecost 8		
70	Wednesday of Holy Week	Wednesday of Holy Week	Wednesday of Holy Week
71:1-6			Epiphany 4
71:1-12	Tuesday of Holy Week	Tuesday of Holy Week	Tuesday of Holy Week
72:1-8	Advent 2		
72:1-14	Epiphany	Epiphany	Epiphany
76	Pentecost 26		
77:11-20			Pentecost 17
78:1-2, 34-38	Holy Cross— September 14 (alternate)	Holy Cross (alternate)	Holy Cross (alternate)
78:1-3, 10-20	Pentecost 13		
80:1-7		Advent 1	Advent 4
81:1-10	Pentecost 20		
82			Pentecost 26
84	Presentation— February 2	Presentation	Presentation
			Pentecost 14
85:8-13		Advent 2	
89:1-4, 19-24		Advent 4	
89:20-21, 24, 26	Maundy Thursday, Chrism service	Maundy Thursday, Chrism service	Maundy Thursday, Chrism service

Index of Psalms for Church Years

Psalm (cont'd)	Year A (cont'd)	Year B (cont'd)	Year C (cont'd)
89:20-37		Pentecost 7	
90:1-12		Pentecost 21	January 1 (New Year)
91:1-10	Pentecost 5		
91:9-16			Lent 1
92:1-4, 12-15			Epiphany 8
93		Pentecost 27	
94:12-22			Pentecost 16
95	Lent 3 Pentecost 14		Pentecost 27
96	Christmas Eve/Day	Christmas Eve/Day	Christmas Eve/Day
97	Christmas Day, Additional, Set 1	Christmas Day, Additional, Set 1	Christmas Day, Additional, Set 1 Easter 7
98	Christmas Day, Additional, Set 2	Christmas Day, Additional, Set 2 Easter 6	Christmas Day, Additional, Set 2
98:1-5	Holy Cross— September 14	Holy Cross	Holy Cross
99	Pentecost 19		Last Sunday After Epiphany
100			Pentecost 2 Thanksgiving Day
101			Pentecost 20
102:1-12		Pentecost 13	
103:1-13	Pentecost 9	Epiphany 8	Lent 3
104:24-34	Pentecost	Pentecost	Pentecost
105:1-11	Pentecost 10	Lent 2	
106:4-12	Pentecost 12		
106:7-8, 19-23	Pentecost 18		
107:1, 33-43			Pentecost 19

Index of Psalms for Church Years

Psalm (cont'd)	Year A (cont'd)	Year B (cont'd)	Year C (cont'd)
107:1-9			Pentecost 18
111	Christmas 1	Christmas 1 Epiphany 4	Christmas 1
112:4-9	Epiphany 5		
113	Visitation—May 31	Visitation	Visitation Pentecost 3
114	Pentecost 15		
115:1-11	Pentecost 16		
116:1-9	Lent 5		
116:12-19	Maundy Thursday	Maundy Thursday	Maundy Thursday
	Easter 3		
117	January 1 (New Year)		
118:14-24	Easter	Easter	Easter
118:19-29	Lent 6, Palm Sunday	Lent 6, Palm Sunday	Lent 6, Palm Sunday
119:1-8	Epiphany 6		
119:33-40	Epiphany 8		
119:33-48		Pentecost 24	
119:129-136		Pentecost 16	
119:137-144			Pentecost 22
121		Pentecost 15	
122	Advent 1		
124	Pentecost 7		
125		Pentecost 17	
126		Pentecost 23	Advent 2
		Thanksgiving Day	Lent 5
127	Pentecost 24		Lent 2
128	Pentecost 23	Pentecost 20	
130	Lent 1		
132:11-18		Pentecost 8	

Index of Psalms for Church Years

Psalm (cont'd)	Year A (cont'd)	Year B (cont'd)	Year C (cont'd)
133		Easter 2	
135:1-14	Pentecost 21		
137:1-6		Lent 4	
138			Epiphany 5
139:1-12			Pentecost 8
139:13-18			Pentecost 9
143:1-8		Pentecost 12	
143:1-10	Pentecost 11		
145:8-13a		Pentecost 26	
145:13b-21			Easter 5
146	Pentecost 22	Pentecost 25	
146:5-10	Advent 3		
147:1-11		Epiphany 5	
147:12-20	Christmas 2	Christmas 2	Christmas 2
149			All Saints—November 1
150	Easter Evening	Easter Evening	Easter Evening